An Asperger Leader's Guide to Living and Le.

of related interest

Asperger's Syndrome Workplace Survival Guide
A Neurotypical's Secrets for Success
Barbara Bissonnette
Foreword by Yvona Fast
ISBN 978 1 84905 943 5
eISBN 978 0 85700 807 7

Managing with Asperger Syndrome
Malcolm Johnson
ISBN 978 1 84310 199 4
eISBN 978 1 84642 029 0

Business for Aspies
42 Best Practices for Using Asperger Syndrome Traits at Work Successfully
Ashley Stanford
ISBN 978 1 84905 845 2
eISBN 978 0 85700 501 4

An Asperger Leader's Guide to

Living and
Leading Change

Rosalind A. Bergemann
Foreword by Will Napier

Jessica Kingsley *Publishers*
London and Philadelphia

Sections of Part 1 and Part 3 have been adapted from Bergemann, R.A. (2007) *Living and Leading Change: A Hands-on Guide to Change Management*. Cranleigh: Scorpcorp Publishing with permission of Scorpcorp Publishing. Extracts also reproduced with permission. Copyright © Rosalind A. Bergemann.

Extracts from Baddeley, S. and James, K. (1987) 'Owl, Fox, Donkey or Sheep: Political skills for managers.' *Management Education & Development 18*, 1, 3–19 reproduced with permission of Simon Baddeley and Kim Turnbull James. Copyright © Simon Baddeley and Kim Turnbull James.

First published in 2014
by Jessica Kingsley Publishers
73 Collier Street
London N1 9BE, UK
and
400 Market Street, Suite 400
Philadelphia, PA 19106, USA

www.jkp.com

Copyright © Rosalind A. Bergemann 2014
Foreword copyright © Will Napier 2014

Front cover image source: iStockphoto®. The cover image is for illustrative purposes only.

Library of Congress Cataloging in Publication Data
A CIP catalog record for this book is available from the Library of Congress

British Library Cataloguing in Publication Data
A CIP catalogue record for this book is available from the British Library

ISBN 978 1 84905 471 3
eISBN 978 0 85700 872 5

Printed and bound in Great Britain

This book is dedicated to all those outstanding individuals
who have overcome the challenge and stigma of
Asperger syndrome
to become leaders within their companies.

It is also dedicated to my daughter Dawn,
without whose love, encouragement and eccentric example
I would not be the person I am today!

Contents

Acknowledgements

Acknowledgements are initially due to all the remarkable fellow Aspergerians I have had the privilege of liaising with as a result of my work with Asperger Leaders.

Acknowledgements are also due to Will Napier for the insights provided into some of the neurotypical interpretations of our Asperger leadership tendencies!

Foreword

My interest in people with Asperger syndrome (AS), or high-functioning autism, began with my interest in the development of the self, a sense of identity. How we see ourselves depends on our context. If everyone was British (and I'm glad they are not!), we wouldn't need the word 'British'. If everyone was neurotypical (and again I'm glad they are not), we wouldn't need this word either. Thanks to the existence of those on the autistic spectrum, we are able to see that being neurotypical (just as being British) is not the only way. It challenges us to see that things that we think of as 'normal' may be quite limited and unimaginative.

The idea of two cultures seems helpful. They can enrich each other, but there are also challenges with communication. Really good translation requires a speaker fluent in both languages, and native speakers to test how natural a translation sounds in the target language. Dr Rosalind Bergemann is someone who is natively Asperger, but who has painstakingly learnt the language of those who are not – the neurotypicals (NTs). I am someone who is natively (perhaps typically) NT and have had the opportunity to learn a different language and perspective through working with many high-functioning AS adults in my London psychology practice. I have had the privilege of working closely with Rosalind over several years in her mission to interpret each group to the other. Through the organisation Asperger Leaders, this hard-won knowledge and understanding is being made available to other AS individuals seeking or finding themselves in leadership positions in business and the professions.

This book is aimed at those with a diagnosis of AS, and those who consider that 'Asperger traits' would be a good way to describe them, whether or not they have a diagnosis. In the years that I have been working closely with AS clients, I have observed that although there can be problems associated with this way of being, there are often enormous strengths, and these are explained in detail in this book. Although NTs often assume that AS people are somehow 'difficult' to work with or relate to, I have found that they are inspiring, challenging, interesting and sometimes downright amusing. It often falls to me to be the one to attempt to explain to an AS person why it is that in order not to appear arrogant, they might have to 'pretend' not to know something, or in order not to appear rude, it might be best to say 'I'm fine' when they are in fact very depressed or anxious, because people aren't usually *really* asking for information about one's wellbeing, but rather establishing an initial rapport for the sake of communication about something else. It is sometimes necessary to 'interpret' the reactions of NTs, for example to explain why it might be that employees reacted with offence when they were told some important bad news by email rather than directly.

I will often mistakenly think that a client is expressing a dark sense of humour – for example, someone who expressed a belief that the only reason why they were successful in their role was because the detail of it was so boring to his colleagues that they wouldn't know whether he was doing a good job or not. However, he was being quite serious, and this led to good conversation about objective evidence for the quality of his work.

It is often thought that AS traits will mean that a person will have to accept that they will never have a leadership role in an organisation, and thus be confined to middle management at the most. My clinical experience shows that in reality AS people often find that their particular strengths not only compensate for their weaknesses, but are so rare and valued that they reach positions on the boards of multinational companies as directors and other senior roles. Rosalind's book does much to detail exactly how and why those with AS can be successful.

However, this is also a book about change. It might perhaps seem comical that Rosalind, being AS herself, has developed international expertise in – of all things – *change*! After all, aren't AS people supposed to find change really difficult? Well yes, of course there are many aspects of AS that make change difficult – the desire for routine and order, the tendency to be very loyal to a person or organisation, the difficulty with interpersonal skills such as communication, empathy and flexibility of approach. However, it is precisely this difficulty with everyday change that forces those with AS to learn exactly the skills they need to excel when there is organisational change, and this is one reason why Rosalind is an expert in coping with change. I have sometimes observed that my role in working with those with AS is often to help 'mine' their own experience and skills from one area of their life, and apply it to work or relationships in a way that hadn't occurred to them. Judging the relevance of things is often a big challenge for those with AS, part of what is known as 'weak central processing' or, in more everyday language, not being able to see the wood for the trees – missing the bigger picture due to the attention to detail (although Rosalind has some interesting things to say about this in Chapter 4).

This book will be a great encouragement to those who are either in, or aspire to take on, leadership roles in business and the professions. I hope it will also be an inspiration and challenge to those NTs who assume that AS people are a liability. The message is loud and clear in these pages: the innate strengths, and the skills you have had to learn in many areas of your life, mean that if you have Asperger traits, you are in some ways even better equipped to adapt than those who have never experienced the challenges of change.

Will Napier
Chartered psychologist in private practice
Harley Street, London

Introduction

When people think about those with autism in the workplace, the sad fact is that many of them consider this to represent a relatively 'lower-level' employee. Even when the concept of 'high-functioning autism' or Asperger syndrome is discussed, the highest consideration that appears to be given to an employee is one who is a computer geek or software programmer stuck behind a monitor all day, hidden from the rest of the organisation.

The reality is that there are a number of very prominent business leaders in the corporate world who have Asperger syndrome. These leaders have learnt to cope with the additional challenges they may have encountered as a result of their developmental disorder – and have succeeded. Yet frequently this success is not recognised due to the fact that these leaders feel the need to hide their diagnosis because of the stigma associated with the term 'autism' and the threat (be it direct or indirect) this may represent for their continued career progression.

Be that as it may, if a person with Asperger syndrome moves into a leadership role in business, one central business occurrence that they are highly likely to face is that of a programme of change. Change programmes – be they smaller change projects or organisation-wide transformation programmes – are an essential element of a leadership role. But for people with Asperger syndrome, this can present the individual with an entirely new situation. They can no longer purely apply previous coping strategies to see them through any obstacles these programmes present them. As a leader, they now need to be able to apply different techniques in order to lead others through those same challenges, and ultimately to be the role model for the people reporting to them. Frequently, this change in emphasis can create significant stress for a person with Asperger syndrome holding a leadership role. It is something that they were not expecting, something they did not have time to prepare new coping strategies for, and something that resulted in reactions arising within themselves that they did not expect and did not understand how to manage.

I would like to open this book with a short scenario of an executive with Asperger syndrome – possibly one that you, if you are a reader with Asperger syndrome holding a senior position in business, can identify with.

Case study: An executive with Asperger syndrome

Robert is what is now defined as a person with high-functioning autism, or Asperger syndrome. This is something he had only been formally diagnosed with in his early 40s, and therefore he had spent most of his life developing his own coping mechanisms to deal with some of the issues this developmental disorder presented him with. Robert had worked diligently at his career over the years and had progressively made his way up the career ladder to the executive position he currently held.

Robert had always been philosophical about his work. Sure, he had experienced challenges – perhaps more than most. Certain parts of the job always seemed to be more difficult for him than it had been for others. It was only after his diagnosis that he came to understand that this was as a result of his Asperger syndrome, and that he wasn't alone in the way his thought patterns differed from most of the people that he worked with. But he had managed to overcome those professional challenges, present a confident and proficient face to the working world and finally step up into the position of Director of Operations in his company.

Things had worked well for him over the years. Yes, there were times when his coping mechanisms needed to be adjusted, but this was something he was learning to do. After all, he had spent his entire life learning how to cope with things. Moving into a leadership role in his organisation presented him with some unique situations that he had not had to face before, but he had managed. That was – he had managed until last year.

At the end of the previous year, a decision had been taken by the Board to acquire a competitor company. Robert had been fully behind this decision, since he was aware that the revenues their combined presence in the marketplace could generate were substantial. In fact, it was Robert who had undertaken the initial market research and due diligence, since the leadership team was well aware of his outstanding ability to delve into detail where necessary and pull together the required facts and figures in a concise and succinct form. The negotiations and discussions between the two parties and their legal teams had taken place and the acquisition was agreed 18 months earlier. Robert had then been nominated as executive sponsor for the integration programme.

Pulling together the programme team and initiating the programme itself had been exciting for Robert. He enjoyed planning and developing project plans, although he was aware that his role was not that of programme manager, but that of sponsor. He appointed a Programme Manager for the transformation programme, and the acquisition process kicked off.

Within four months of the programme starting, however, Robert noticed that he was starting to experience more stress than usual, although he was not able specifically to identify the reason for the tension. Aware of the fact that this could be as a result of his Asperger syndrome, Robert tried to review any areas in his work environment where he could be experiencing problems, but with no real insights. He had identified that some of his staff were communicating with him in a slightly different way, but he struggled to work out how. Recognising facial expressions and body language had never been his strong point, and in addition he often missed what others felt were blatantly obvious clues in written communication as well. He struggled to understand why people who had consistently been key performers in his team were now falling behind on their targets, and sometimes even failing to do what he asked them.

Robert also noticed that he was starting to experience far more sensory overload than he had for quite a while. He had made the decision not to advise his employers about his Asperger syndrome when he was diagnosed, concerned at how they might react. Now, however, he was struggling to sit in meetings held in rooms with fluorescent lighting, or hold programme workshops in large open-plan areas where the noise levels were now uncomfortable for him. He longed to shut himself away in an office, but the result of the integration had been the loss of dedicated office space and a conversion to open-plan offices. Suddenly his coping routine just didn't fit into the pace of work he found himself involved with, and he had little time to step back and find other solutions.

Robert also noticed that there appeared to be some sort of issue with the leadership team in respect of his handling of the programme. They seemed to be raising issues with him that he could not see as being a problem, or sometimes not even saying anything to him directly, but rather complaining to others in the leadership team who then passed the information on to him.

After another few months, Robert found that his workload had more than doubled. He was becoming more and more intrinsically involved with the programme management – and even project management – elements of the acquisition programme; and due to some of the challenges he had experienced from the leadership team, he had insisted that all decisions in respect of the programme go through him first. At the same time, he had tried to delegate more of his business-as-usual responsibilities to his deputy, but she was becoming uncooperative and not meeting deadlines. Robert felt that this programme was starting to smother him, and began to experience anxiety attacks.

The final straw for Robert came when he started to recognise that his team, who had previously worked with him so well, were becoming openly antagonistic towards him – or so he felt. Again, recognising emotions or bodily language had always been something he needed to work at, and he appeared to be misinterpreting people more and more of late. Perhaps this company was better off without him and his shortcomings.

The person described above may be fictional, but the situation in which he found himself is one that a number of people with Asperger syndrome have experienced themselves. Change programmes can be challenging for any business leader, but for those of us who have Asperger syndrome, the difficulties can be significantly more complex. Key to that increased complexity is that frequently we are not even aware of the fact that new issues have arisen, or that our current coping mechanisms are not working optimally in this new scenario.

The aim of this book is to assist those business leaders with Asperger syndrome to successfully lead and personally cope with change programmes within their organisations, both as leaders and as individuals. This book is written specifically for you as a person with Asperger syndrome holding a senior position in business; a person who has already developed coping mechanisms to help you succeed in your career to date; a person who wants to continue to grow your career and not be hindered by the new challenges a change programme will present you with.

The examples and case studies in this book are taken from the experiences of people who have found themselves in situations that may be similar to your own, and I present this to you as someone who has experienced these same challenges herself as an Asperger leader.

I encourage you make use of the tools and exercises available to you in this book to assist you in continuing in your career development.

PART 1

The Change Life-cycle and How that Affects Us as Leaders with Asperger Syndrome

Chapter 1

Defining the Asperger Leadership Challenge

Making the move up the career ladder from middle management to senior management and ultimately to the leadership team in an organisation is the objective of most serious business people, and the day they finally make that step can come as an incredible vindication of time, effort and dedication on their part to date.

For those of us who have Asperger syndrome, that achievement is often even more personally satisfying. For years, we have been working our way up the same career ladder as our peers, but we have done so with an inherent shortfall in some of the critical skill areas intuitively expected of managers and leaders – communication skills, networking skills, political skills, negotiation skills. We are wired differently. These are skills we are not naturally imbued with, but we have managed to develop strategies either to learn to encompass these skills with some additional work on our side, or to find ways of managing around these requirements. In some ways, I like to think of it as our learning to lead in an environment which focuses on hearing skills when we ourselves are deaf. Sure, we may not hear exactly what they are saying, but we have learnt sophisticated techniques to adapt, such as lip-reading, having audio-translation machines available, and so forth.

No matter what the challenge, we tend to find the solution. After all, many of us have – without realising it – already learnt this skill even at school, when our differences made the environment hostile or challenging. Every person has his or her own coping strategies that have been successful in helping them reach the top (or higher rungs!) of their own individual career ladder.

As you step into your leadership role, you may be confident that this is a role you will handle without any issues, or you could be concerned with what new challenges the role may present you with that you – perhaps – are not familiar with, or have never faced. So what are some of the key differences between a management role and a senior management or leadership role within an organisation, and what implications are there for you as an individual with Asperger syndrome?

Leadership skills versus management skills

In order to understand the implications for us, I should start by clarifying what I mean by management skills versus leadership skills.

Kotter's model of Leadership

A very concise description of the difference between management skills and leadership skills is provided by John Kotter (1996). Kotter identified three key elements of management versus leadership (Table 1.1).

Table 1.1 Management skills versus leadership skills

Management skills	Leadership skills
Planning and organising	Setting a direction
Organising and managing resources	Aligning people to a vision
Controlling and problem solving	Motivating and inspiring

Let us break this brief summary down a little further.

PLANNING AND ORGANISING

I believe most of us can identify with this requirement for management. We need to develop plans and budgets, we need to organise the work in our departments and teams, we need to ensure that the work is done. It can include the development of policies and procedures, as well as ensuring that these are adhered to. Whilst many people with Asperger's initially experience challenges with tasks such as prioritisation, by the time we have moved into management we will have established effective strategies to make these effective for us.

ORGANISING AND MANAGING RESOURCES

This is one of the areas where Asperger managers can face an ongoing challenge. This skill covers not only organising and managing the requirements for the department or team in respect of physical resources such as IT equipment, capital budget and so forth, but also includes the development of the staffing structure of the team, and managing the human resource requirements and needs. In effect, it includes the 'managing people' part of the job.

CONTROLLING AND PROBLEM SOLVING

By this, Kotter was referring to the requirement for the manager to keep an eye on operations, identify any issues arising and ensure they are resolved. This is an essential part of the 'business as usual' part of management. I believe this is an area where we, as people with Asperger syndrome, tend to perform well. We have the natural ability to notice very quickly when things are not optimal and when there are things appearing that should not be there. It is also acknowledged that we tend to be very creative in our area of expertise, largely due to the voluminous amount of information we generally hold in our heads about our area of speciality.

Summarising the above, we can see that a manager is someone who is responsible for planning, organising, controlling and problem solving. These are areas within which we, as individuals with Asperger syndrome, tend to excel. We naturally lean towards organisation and planning, and tend to be very good at controlling resources (albeit that human resources may be a little more of a challenge!). Of course, this is a generalisation, and certainly there will be some people on the autistic spectrum who find controlling and problem solving challenging, or managing people easy.

If we look at the above breakdown, what we are also seeing is that the manager is largely focused on predictability and order, keeping things running as they should, making sure they fit the parameters. Keeping control. Maintaining order. Avoiding unwanted change. Sounds appealing, doesn't it?

Now let's examine Kotter's criteria for leadership.

SETTING A DIRECTION

Leaders are people who develop a vision for the organisation or for the division they lead. They also are responsible for developing a related strategy to achieve that vision. As an Asperger leader, this may not be too much of a challenge for you. In fact, you may find it incredibly motivating to be able to develop a vision for the organisation, since frequently those of us with Asperger syndrome can visualise different states of an organisation quite readily, and thereby have a good idea of where the company needs to go to be successful.

ALIGNING PEOPLE TO A VISION

Well, perhaps this is where some people with Asperger's may pause. Aligning people to a vision obviously entails communicating your vision in such a way that it inspires and motivates the entire workforce (or the entire division, should this be the case). The leader needs to be able to ensure that the vision is understood, internalised and acted on by everyone. He or she needs to be the one to drive the ownership of the vision by the employees.

MOTIVATING AND INSPIRING

Some people wonder if this criterion isn't really just part of the previous one – after all, don't you align people by motivating and inspiring them? The answer is that the difference here is the context in which the motivation and inspiration requirements arise. Aligning people to a vision means getting people to understand, accept and take ownership of a group vision. The motivation and inspiration requirement from the leader refers to the requirement to introduce change into the organisation, and to use motivation and inspiration to overcome any barriers to that change.

EXECUTIVE INTELLIGENCE

More recent research into organisational behaviour and the psychology of leadership has also emphasised the importance of what is known as 'executive intelligence'. According to Menkes (2005), key skills for executives can be categorised under the headings of task, people and self. These are further detailed as follows:

1. Accomplish tasks, utilising various cognitive skills, including:

   - Critically examining underlying assumptions
   - Identifying probably unintended consequences
   - Distinguishing primary goals from less relevant concerns
   - Anticipating probable outcomes
   - Recognising people's underlying agendas.

2. Working with and through others, utilising people skills, including:

   - Recognising the underlying agendas of others
   - Considering the probable effects of one's actions
   - Recognising personal biases or limitations in your own perspectives
   - Pursuing feedback that may reveal an error in judgement and making appropriate judgements.

3. Judge yourself and adapt your behaviour accordingly, using behaviours such as:

- Seeking out and using feedback

- Recognising when it is appropriate to stand your ground and resist the arguments of others

- Acknowledging personal errors and mistakes.

EMOTIONAL INTELLIGENCE

Another element that organisational psychologists have identified as crucial to successful leadership is the linkage to what is called 'emotional intelligence' (Cooper and Sawaf 1998; Goleman, Boyatzis and McKee 2002; Stein and Book 2000). Stein and Book (2000) identify five realms of emotional intelligence, namely:

1. *Intrapersonal* (self-awareness, actualisation, independence, self-regard)

2. *Interpersonal* (empathy, social responsibility)

3. *Adaptability* (problem solving, flexibility)

4. *Stress Management* (stress tolerance, impulse control)

5. *General Mood* (happiness, optimism).

Looking at the above leadership skills, it should be apparent that the focus of leadership is change – new visions, new strategies, new direction. It is the opposite of predictability and order; it is change and risk. You should also be able to see that leadership focuses on some very different types of skill as opposed to those of management, some of which include:

- Strong written and verbal communication skills

- Strong interpersonal skills to listen to and hear what it is people are really saying

- Ability to read situations and underlying messages and politics

- Motivational skills to encourage people to take ownership of the vision and associated changes

- Negotiation skills to deal with individuals or groups with differing options

- Conflict management skills to handle any tensions or friction

- Risk-taking skills to be able to take a visible stand for new ideas and changes

- Stress management and the ability to control emotions

- Understanding of self and how you work optimally

- Ability to seek feedback proactively and adapt your behaviours as appropriate.

I am certain that most people with Asperger syndrome can acknowledge that the above list includes some of the activities that can potentially be the most daunting for us. However, these are the main focus of your role as leader. It is important to recognise that elements of the management skills you have used so successfully to date will remain with you, especially where you have a direct team reporting to you and a budget to control. However, the most significant part of your role now relates to interpersonal and communication-related skills.

This is where the Asperger leadership challenge lies. I like to think of this as a positive challenge, and not a negative one, since I know of many people who are outstanding leaders and who also have Asperger syndrome. But it is certainly an area that we need to ensure we are aware of and where we need to take the necessary leadership development steps to ensure our optimal performance. This book focuses on the change management element of the leadership development challenge, and aims to provide some useful tools for you to use in order to ensure that you can confidently and successfully lead change in your organisation.

Chapter 2

Examining the Psychological Contract

Over the last few years both public and private sector organisations have continued to review their strategies in order to remain competitive and achieve targets set or expected of them by their customers and stakeholders. The result has been ongoing change initiatives, and seemingly endless re-engineering, restructuring and reorganisation.

Change management is a subject which is very topical at the moment – understandably so, if we take the above into consideration. Numerous books have been written on the subject, specialists hold seminars regularly and change-management consultants are busier than ever.

Yet despite this obvious focus on the topic, many change-management programmes fail dismally, despite the company ensuring the recruitment of the best programme managers, the appointment of the highest paid consultants and the development of the most complex and specific project plans. How can this be?

Defining change

When I have asked some of my clients to share with me their definition of a change programme, many company directors and CEOs have frowned and fixed me with a strange expression, as if to question why I would be asking them such a fundamental question.

However, the reality is that whilst the majority of these clients were well able to define change programmes in terms of strategy, project management and corporate management policy, very few included the human side of change in their description.

I always make the point at this stage that I personally do not agree with the term 'change management'. As far as I am concerned, that is a contradiction in terms. We know from our discussion on the differences between management and leadership that management relates to business as usual, utilising established procedures and maintaining order and process. Of course, this just isn't compatible with the concept of change, where we are working on something that is likely to interfere with business as usual – albeit temporarily, altering established procedures and creating new processes.

The concept of 'change management' implies the controlling of change in such a way as to make it orderly, structured and process driven. Effectively, when senior managers visualise change, they are frequently thinking of this side of change – the change *management* side. But a change programme involves far more than change management; it involves the change process, the human factors and the changes to the psychological contract with employees in the company. Change can most effectively be thought of as a living, breathing, adapting creature – hence my description of the change life-cycle.

So let's take a step back and review the definition of change after making the following key considerations central:

- A change programme is dependent on a change occurring in your company and its system of operation; the operations of your company are dependent on the people who work within it.

- A programme of change is going to have the most dramatic effect on the people who work in your company.

- The majority of people react negatively to changes which alter their accepted way of life – either in the workplace or outside it.

Logic tells us, therefore, that any sort of change programme is intrinsically linked to the management of your employees' experience of the process.

Change and the human factor

A major factor in the shortcomings of a number of change programmes is a lack of understanding of the human factor in the change process – not only the human factor in respect of a leader's employees, but also the human factor associated with the leader him- or herself.

Times of change, more than any other time in the employment life-cycle, are when an understanding of the psychology of the individual and the sociology of the team is invaluable.

The purpose of this book is to address the issue of the human factor in change whilst not overlooking the practical side of the exercise in the process. We walk through some of the critical elements of the psychological contract in the employment relationship, and consider what the effects of change are for both you as a leader and those you lead.

We will then review 12 key skills identified as being utilised by those who have led successful change programmes in their companies, be it at organisation, departmental or functional level.

The psychological contract

Central to the employment relationship is the psychological contract. For leaders with Asperger syndrome, the psychological contract can present a challenge, not only in recognising the intrinsic nature of the contract, but in being able to identify any shifts that may be happening within that contract as a result of changes in the organisation. Let us first start by more formally identifying what we mean by the term 'psychological contract'.

Perhaps the most concise definition is to say that the psychological contract is an unwritten document, implying a set of mutual expectations and needs as a result of the employment relationship (Schein 1988).

Employees have expectations in respect of such things as job security, fair pay, development opportunities, a good working environment, and so forth. This is their psychological contract with their employer. On the other side, the employer has expectations in respect of loyalty of the employee to the organisation, commitment of the employee to undertake his or her work to the best of their ability, to uphold the image of the organisation, not to betray the trust the company has placed in them, and so on.

Whilst the above description appears straightforward, there is another, less formally specified element to the psychological contract with which we, as leaders with Asperger syndrome, sometimes grapple. This is the actual *psychological* part of that contract – the mind-sets of the people involved, the feelings induced by the ownership of the contract, the emotions stirred by changes to the contract, and the necessity to recognise and deal with those reactions. In general, those of us with Asperger syndrome have a shortcoming in what is called 'theory of mind'. Theory of mind is the ability to attribute mental states – beliefs, intents, desires, pretending, knowledge, and so forth – to oneself and others and to understand that others have beliefs, desires and intentions that are different from our own. Having a theory of mind allows one to predict or explain other people's actions, and enables us to understand that mental states can be the cause of – and therefore be used to explain and predict – other people's behaviour (Gordon 1996). It has been recognised that people with Asperger syndrome, especially high-functioning Asperger syndrome, have generally taught themselves to deal with this shortcoming through intellectual analysis, rote learning and memory as a result of their being unable to achieve this skill intuitively (Attwood 2007). By the time we have reached the level of business social interaction that is required for a management or leadership role, we generally would not be identified by people in the company as having a significant shortfall in this area. In fact, many people with Asperger syndrome have careers in fields which require regular contact with people and the need for a degree of awareness of 'what people are thinking'. Despite this, when there are changes to an organisation that affect that individual – directly or indirectly – very often this creates new, unfamiliar scenarios where previously operational 'theory of mind coping mechanisms' may no longer be sufficient.

For this reason, I have included this chapter early in the book to ensure that you as a leader of change are better equipped adequately to identify and recognise any psychological effects on your employees of a change programme you may be leading.

If we are going to initiate a change programme within an organisation, it is critical to understand that no matter how seemingly small or short the change programme is scheduled to be, this action has the potential negatively to affect the psychological contract between the employee and the employer. In the same way that we, as people with Asperger syndrome, can sometimes 'over-react' to changes or adjustments to our environment over which we have no control, people with a psychological contract of any sort will react negatively to changes to this, even if they are ultimately positive.

This is best explained by Sims (1994) who stated:

> A balanced psychological contract is necessary for a continuing, harmonious relationship between the employee and the organization. However, the violation of the psychological contract can signal to the participants that the parties no longer share (or ever shared) a common set of values or goals. (p.378)

What is important for you to understand is that when people believe that their position in the company has changed in some way, they may feel challenged or even threatened. Even though a psychological contract is not an actual written contract, and even if a change to it does not represent a *physical* change in the person's employment or role in the company, it will still be perceived by that person as a change. As a result, it is highly likely that the individual's attitudes, emotions and visible behaviours will change. You saw in my introduction the fictional Director of Operations, Robert, experiencing a challenge in respect of his staff, and his inability to understand what was changing. Reading through this chapter, it should make it easier for you to identify that the changes he was witnessing (if not comprehending) were directly related to the changes in the psychological contract experienced by his team.

So what do we need to understand about the psychological contract? Let's start by looking at the employment situation from the individual's point of view.

Individual needs and expectations

When individuals start working for a company, there are a number of expectations that will be important to them. Each individual will have certain expectations that are unique to him or her, such as expecting to have the opportunity to be trained into a specialist position within two years, or to receive an upper quartile salary. However, there will also be a number of shared expectations, such as the expectation of continued employment and the expectation of a regular salary, for example. Whether the individual's expectations are unique or shared, they can ultimately be classified into three specific categories: financial, social and intrinsic (see Figure 2.1).

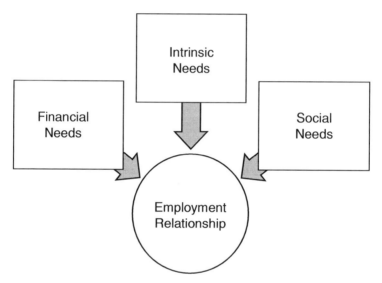

Figure 2.1 Needs and expectations of individuals in the employment relationship

These needs or expectations are the core of the individual's working relationship with the employer. They are integral to determining how the individual feels about what their employer is offering them and how much they want to give back in return. I will not focus in this chapter on the financial element of the psychological contract. I am certain that as a leader in your business you are already well aware of the needs of people in respect of their salaries and benefits. However, what is equally, if not more, important for a large number of people are the elements of intrinsic and social needs.

For those of us who do not have the same 'socially focused' mind-set as most neurotypicals, the importance of the social environment can sometimes be undermined. For the majority of people, their relationships within the company are central to their work experience. They develop friendships and social networks in the organisation, and changes that may disrupt this can have a very detrimental effect on their motivation and desire to stay with the company.

Similarly, when we hear people speak about the intrinsic needs of people in the company, this may be difficult for us to conceptualise. As mentioned earlier, a weakness in the area of theory of mind can mean that we sometimes assume that if we feel a certain way about something, everyone else will. Let us consider an example to help illustrate the point.

Case study: Not reading the signs

Katie is Managing Director of a multinational company headquartered in Cambridge undergoing a significant change programme. She has not led the programme of change directly, but has made attempts to drive the programme through the organisation by making presentations to the employees, by doing roadshows, and by ensuring that all her direct reports are given the opportunity to share in some of the most exciting elements of the change. One day, whilst preparing for a presentation at one of the company's satellite offices, she decides to give one of her managers the opportunity to lead the presentation rather than doing it herself, feeling that she should be sharing this exciting experience with the manager concerned. After the presentation, Katie enters the ladies room to find her manager there in floods of tears. Taken aback, she leaves the restroom, since she does not know what is wrong with her manager or how to handle it. Later that day, her personal assistant updates her on the manager's state of mind. It turns out that the manager had been against the changes being initiated right from the start, and also had a fear of public speaking.

Another point made by Katie's PA was that the manager concerned had been trying to let her know there was a problem through her body language and facial expressions. Katie's PA made the comment, 'Surely you must have seen the look on her face when you asked her to make the presentation?' Katie was surprised, responding that she had seen the look on her face – but that she thought she had looked pleased and excited. Her PA laughed and retorted, 'Katie, if looks could kill...' Katie went back to her work, concerned at what her PA had told her, and feeling insecure about her ability to work positively with her manager going forward.

The above example reflects a number of challenges that we, as Asperger leaders, can be faced with. When Katie had decided to delegate the presentation to her direct report, she had assumed that because she was excited about the programme, enjoyed presentations and wanted to represent the company at roadshows, her team members did as well. That is an example of what is called 'mindblindness' (Baron-Cohen 1995), where we just do not recognise that people aren't necessarily on the same 'page' as us. Because of this Katie was not attuned to the intrinsic needs of her direct report. She had (due to mindblindness) assumed that this person shared the same intrinsic needs as herself. Her PA highlighted that this obviously was not the case – the manager did not agree with the change and certainly did not support it. However, she was being 'forced' publicly to give the programme her perceived backing. In all likelihood, this employee felt that Katie was aware of her misgivings about the change programme, and was trying to put her in a situation where she had to show her support of the change, whether she liked it or not. Of course, this was not Katie's intention. However, this was the impression that was given due to Katie's inability to recognise her manager's emotions accurately. In addition, this example highlights a related challenge that we frequently face, namely difficulties with the accurate recognition of emotions, body language and facial expressions. Katie had been sufficiently aware of her subordinate's facial expression to recognise that there had been a change when she told her to do the presentation. However, Katie had misinterpreted it as excitement, not recognising it as annoyance, resentment or anger, as other people obviously were able to.

In short, the psychological contract can be the focus of the emotions and attitudes of the employee, which will have a direct effect on his or her behaviour (Spindler 1994).

We know that increasing pressures for organisations to change in order to become more competitive has caused disillusionment with the traditional psychological contract, historically based on expectations of lifelong employment and steady internal progression (Hiltrop 1996). Guest *et al.* (1996) emphasise that employees continue to expect what they have always expected – job security, a career, fair pay, and so on – but employers no longer feel obliged to provide this. In fact, employers are actually expecting greater and greater levels of performance from their employees, despite situations of change and uncertainty, whilst offering them less in return – not necessarily financially, but in terms of the psychological contract itself.

The end result of the unspoken change in the psychological contract is confusion and frustration on the part of the employee, which has a direct effect on motivation. This loss of motivation will ultimately lead to one of two types of behaviour: constructive behaviour or frustration and its associated negative responses (Mullins 1999).

Negative responses associated with an employee's frustration will be discussed further in Chapters 17–19, but the four main types of behaviour identified by Mullins are aggression, regression, fixation and withdrawal. Without going into the details of these types of behaviour at this stage, it should be easy to see why it is so important to ensure that people undergoing change have their energies channelled in the right direction, namely constructive behaviour.

As I mentioned earlier in the chapter, a change in the psychological contract is bound to occur as a result of a change programme. What you need to ensure, as a leader of people and a leader of change, is that the contract is re-established along solid principles as a result of your handling of the change process. What you additionally need to ensure, as a leader with Asperger syndrome, is that you develop and have in place strategies to recognise when a change could be affecting a psychological contract as well as when people's attitudes are changing. Additionally, it is important to recognise that you yourself are likely to face changes to your own psychological contract that you may find stressful or challenging. These are likely to differ significantly from those employees who do not have Asperger's. What is important for you is to be aware of what sort of changes to the psychological contract are more Asperger-related, understand how this could affect you and learn the signals to be able to recognise when this is happening so that you can take appropriate action to get your stresses under control and coping strategies working. This will be covered in detail in Chapter 4.

The rest of this book focuses on how you can prepare both yourself and your team for the changes to come, as well as detailing some key skills that should assist you in ensuring that your change programme is a success.

Chapter 3

Understanding the Psychological Change Cycle

Before I begin speaking about the specifics of how change is going to affect you and your people, let us spend a little time having a look at the root cause of some of those effects – the psychological change cycle.

Whilst this is certainly not intended to be a book focusing on psychology, by the very nature of what we are covering as we discuss change it would be impossible to provide insight into how to help people successfully through change if we do not enter the realms of the human psyche. In addition, as leaders with Asperger syndrome, we know this is potentially a problem area for us, since understanding the psychology of others requires some degree of insight as well as empathy. This chapter is a broad outline of the psychological change cycle, provided with the intention of giving you some insight prior to looking at how to apply this to yourself, as well as understanding how it affects others.

Several psychologists have done research in the field of the change cycle for the individual, both as a general occurrence and as an event within an organisational environment. Key to this research is the understanding that change is often related to some kind of trauma. That may sound surprising to you, but if you think about it, change generally involves some sort of loss – be it the loss of something tangible (such as the death of a loved one, the loss of a job, the loss of an office) or the loss of something intangible (loss of security, loss of confidence, loss of privacy). Elisabeth Kübler-Ross undertook research into the effects of loss as a result of death or finding out about a terminal illness (Kübler-Ross 1969). This initial research showed that people go through five stages of emotional coping: denial, anger, bargaining, depression and acceptance. The results were built on by a number of other researchers (Adams, Hayes and Hopson 1976; Bergemann 2007; Satir *et al.* 1991; Weinberg 1997) to develop a broader change curve reflecting how people progress through the phases of change relative to their performance in the company. Each identified phase is distinct and has differing effects on both the individual and those around them. Whilst I am not going to go into the detail of the curve itself, I do think it is important to understand the phases themselves and their effects. It is these effects that are of interest to us as leaders of change.

So what are these phases of the psychological change cycle and how do they manifest themselves in people's behaviour? There are a relatively large number of phases in a psychological change cycle. In order to more effectively understand them, I have categorised these according to how people progress through the transitional process. The transitional process is the personal, individual journey that a person going through change needs to take in order to complete the psychological adjustment. These transitional stages provide the emotional and psychological framework for the 13 phases of the psychological change cycle.

The transitional stages and phases of the psychological change cycle

I consider there to be four stages to the transitional process linked to an active change cycle: Introversion; Analysis; Acceptance and testing; and Resolution or regression. As mentioned, these provide the framework for 13 phases of the psychological change cycle. The first ten phases are: Shock/numbness; Denial; Defensive blaming; Panic/dread; Depression/insecurity; Contemplation; Acknowledgement; Experimentation; Discovery/learning; and Reflection. After this, there are two potential routes for the change cycle to take, and these are reflected in the options for the remaining three phases, namely: Feelings of optimism/hope versus uncertainty/concern; Feelings of satisfaction versus dissatisfaction; and finally Integration and new meaning versus withdrawal.

The above may appear to be a lot to take in – and I agree – but these phases can be better understood by putting them into the context of the transitional stages, as in Figure 3.1.

An understanding of these transitional stages and the related phases of the psychological change cycle are very important for us to be able to recognise and deal with some of the behaviours that employees may display during your change programme. Whereas most neurotypicals would be able to recognise associated behaviours relatively easily once they know what they are looking for, for us this may require more focus.

Let us start by examining the transitional stages and phases of the psychological change cycle to understand what actually occurs during these periods.

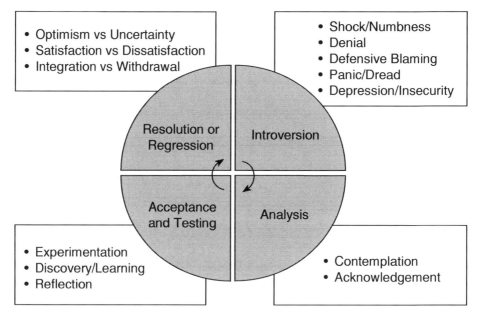

Figure 3.1 Transitional stages and phases of the psychological change cycle

Transitional Stage 1: Introversion

The first stage of the transitional process is very inwardly focused. All of an individual's concerns and perceptions are focused on how the change or situation is going to affect them personally and how they personally feel at the time. They tend not to think about others or the organisation as a whole. The focus is on themselves.

There are five phases of the psychological change cycle that fall within this transitional stage. It is important to understand that some of these phases may overlap or occur in a different order. However, Phases 1 and 5 tend to consistently be the first and last occurrences in this stage respectively.

PHASE 1: SHOCK/NUMBNESS

This occurs when the individual is first exposed to the change or the information that change is coming. At this time the person will often feel shocked and numb, and their ability to rationalise will often be compromised, especially if the event is a significant one.

PHASE 2: DENIAL

In Phase 2, a person tends to play down the pending change or deny the need for it. Typical comments during this phase would be 'That doesn't apply to me', 'It won't affect my role' or 'They're just talking about it – it won't really happen.' Very often a person in this phase of the psychological change cycle will ridicule or undermine people who are further along the cycle.

PHASE 3: DEFENSIVE BLAMING

When an individual reaches this phase of the change cycle, they are starting to realise that something is happening that is not comfortable. The response is anger, generally directed at other people, a particular person, the department, the company. The person is not really aware of the exact reason for their extreme anger and resentment, hence their need to blame someone. Frequently, this will also include blaming oneself: 'I'm such a fool! If I had paid more attention I would have seen this coming' or 'This is all happening because I wasn't able to bring in those big contracts last month.'

PHASE 4: PANIC/DREAD

Once the initial anger and defensive blaming has begun to wear off, people tend to be left with a feeling of anxiety. Something is coming, something uncomfortable, and most people will not know exactly where they stand. The level of anxiety the person experiences can vary from a sense of dread to a feeling of full panic. This is the time when the individual feels most vulnerable and alone. This is the phase where the greatest levels of stress are experienced, and is very often when people make the decision to leave a company.

PHASE 5: DEPRESSION AND INSECURITY

Phase 5 kicks in when a person begins to realise that the change really is happening and that they are – effectively – helpless to stop it. It is often associated with a sense of loss – loss of security, loss of the way things were, perhaps loss of something tangible. People begin to feel apathetic and lose the enthusiasm either to fight the change or to work with it.

TRANSITIONAL STAGE 2: ANALYSIS

The second stage of the transitional process begins when the individual starts to look outward after having been inwardly focused during Stage 1. This begins to occur when the person realises that the change is happening and that it is necessary for them to adapt to it. Effectively, the person looks up and asks, 'What is happening? What are others doing? What do I need to do?'

There are two phases of the psychological change cycle falling within this transitional stage.

PHASE 6: CONTEMPLATION

The individual moves out of his or her stage of depression and begins to take more notice of what is happening around them, considering how this is affecting them. As part of that contemplation, the person will start to recognise that the previous ways of working or life they were familiar with is no longer something they should be focusing on. This is a critical step, since it is the realisation that there is no going back that finally moves the individual into Phase 7.

PHASE 7: ACKNOWLEDGEMENT

Here the individual begins to consider not only the reality of the change taking place, but also their role in it. Unlike the previous phase, during Phase 7 – although an individual may not fully accept the change – they are beginning to play a more active role in considering how they can be part of the change, and what their role might look like going forward compared to how it looks now or in the recent past.

Transitional Stage 3: Acceptance and testing

In Stage 3, the individual makes a significant step forward in the transition process. There is a shift in mind-set whereby the pending change is accepted as a reality, and he or she starts to put into action some of the strategies and action plans being considered in the stage of analysis. One of the most significant indicators of this stage being reached is that the individual starts to identify with the future rather than the past.

PHASE 8: EXPERIMENTATION

People begin to try out new behaviours, or undertake project work to formalise the change. Individuals are trying things out to see if this can work, testing to see if it is genuine and concrete.

PHASE 9: DISCOVERY/LEARNING

Part of the ongoing change and embedding of the new processes is that people continue to learn and grow. It is only by growing into their new roles and the changes now established in the business that this will ultimately become integrated.

PHASE 10: REFLECTION

Once the change has been put into place, or is reaching maturity, people begin to think about the changes that have occurred in more detail and try to understand how it came about and the effect it had on them as individuals. Reflection is the first step towards internalising the new situation – it is the process of personalising it apart from the very strong emotions experienced in Stages 1–3. How an individual is guided through and deals with this phase is critical to whether Phase 13 will be one of internalisation or one of withdrawal.

Transitional Stage 4: Resolution or regression

Stage 4 of the transition process is the only one with two potential routes and ultimate outcomes – internalisation or withdrawal. What determines which of the two routes an individual follows is largely determined by their experiences within Stage 3, especially during the phase of reflection. However, it should be understood that just because an individual has started down one path in the process does not mean that they are committed to this. Their ongoing experiences during this period can make the difference between their continuing on the path they have started on or moving to the alternative one. We can therefore say that each of the phases of the psychological change cycle in this stage are interlinked. This is illustrated in Figure 3.2.

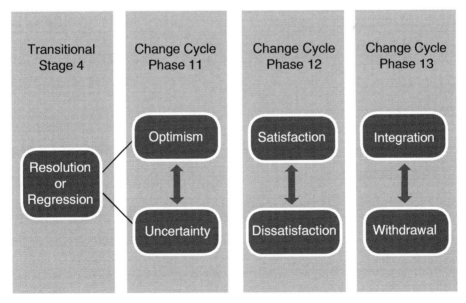

Figure 3.2 Transitional Stage 4 and related phases of the psychological change cycle

PHASE 11: OPTIMISM VERSUS UNCERTAINTY

On the positive route within this phase, an individual will find that they are becoming optimistic and enthusiastic about their new situation. Challenges they have faced appear to have been overcome or are seen as surmountable, with a positive outcome.

On the negative route, an individual finds that they are beginning to feel uncomfortable with the new situation. They start to experience the feeling of not quite fitting in, and being unsettled with the sense of uncertainty.

PHASE 12: SATISFACTION VERSUS DISSATISFACTION

On the positive route within this phase, the person feels that the change has been purposeful and successful. They start to look to the future and focus on their continued growth in the company.

On the negative route, the person begins to feel that the change has had a negative impact on his or her life and starts to regret the effort that has been extended. They will tend to start dwelling on the way things were, or focusing on the way they think things should be.

PHASE 13: INTEGRATION VERSUS WITHDRAWAL

On the positive route within this phase, an individual will have fully integrated the new situation into his or her life. They have been able to make a personal connection to either the change itself or the new situation as a result of their journey through earlier phases and reflection. As a result, they accept the post-change environment as their current and future situation, and any losses associated with the past are forgotten or overcome.

On the negative route, an individual finds that t,hey reject the changes and withdraw from the situation. Regression may result in the failure of a change programme, or at least in the need to undertake a significant 're-education' or 'refresher' programme down the line.

Reading through the above descriptions of the various phases of the psychological change cycle should provide you with some – perhaps familiar – insights into the way change can affect people emotionally and psychologically. In Chapters 4 and 5 I elaborate on this information to provide some more insight into why we react to change the way we do, as well as how you can expect your neurotypical employees to react.

Chapter 4

Understanding How Change Affects You

It is interesting that the majority of books dealing with change focus on dealing with how *other* people deal with and handle change, and yet never really address the very obvious fact that we as leaders – at whatever level that may be – also have to deal with how change affects us personally.

There is no doubt that change does affect us as leaders – especially those of us who are leaders with Asperger syndrome. No matter how positively we may see the change as being, or how well you believe you understand the changes to come, a change programme will have reciprocal effects on us which we need to be aware of and understand how to deal with.

In raising the issue of how change affects people who actually lead or drive change directly, I have often had the response from clients that their personal reactions to change are not very relevant to the way change is managed in the organisation. I must reiterate what I said in Chapter 3, that at times like this, individuals are talking about the concept of change *management* rather than the broader issue of the full *transitional change process*. In reality, their reaction to change is far more important than they realise, and can make the difference between the success and failure of a change programme in a company.

Another reason why it is important to understand how change affects you is that in doing so, it will give you invaluable insights into how the uncertainties and insecurities of change could be affecting those people you will be leading through the same change process. Being aware of your own reactions to change and the insecurities it brings will allow you to develop a critical empathy with the people you are directing – something that we frequently do not develop ourselves without guidance. If your change programme is to be successful, this is an essential skill you will need to develop, since you will be making use of it on a regular basis.

Before we go into a more detailed analysis of how a change programme is going to affect you individually as a leader with Asperger syndrome, I would like to open with a very broad outline of some of the recognised reasons why we tend to be more strongly affected by the stress caused by change.

How do people with Asperger syndrome generally react to stress?

I must start by saying that I believe that this is a highly personal and individually variable topic. The way stress affects one person with Asperger syndrome could differ considerably from the way it affects another. However, what I am looking at in this section are some of the generic causes for any challenges we may experience. Remember that the degree to which these apply to you depends on how well you currently cope with stress, how much exposure you have had to it in the past, and some of your individual sensory and cognitive challenges/strengths.

Sensory overload

Most of us with Asperger syndrome have one or more hypersensitivities. For anyone who is not aware of what this is, this means that we have one or more overly sensitive perceptive senses, be it hearing, eyesight, smell, touch or taste, which are subject to overload due to too much input (Attwood 2007). Unlike neurotypicals, when we start to receive too much input to one of our hypersensitive senses, this creates a build-up of tension ultimately ending in an overload experience. When I first tried to understand how this differed from neurotypicals, the one thing that I realised after speaking to people was that, for a neurotypical, removing oneself from an environment that was uncomfortable resulted in the discomfort immediately ceasing. For example, if someone turned on the radio and it was playing painfully loud, all they needed to do was turn the volume down and then things would be back to normal. For us, however, we are generally not so fortunate. Let's take the same example. We turn on a radio and the volume is painfully loud. We immediately turn off the radio, but the pain and sensation of those voluminous sound-waves continue to resound through us for an hour before they finally dissipate.

I like to visualise this as what I call the 'funnel' effect. Neurotypicals have an open channel through which they can receive sensory information (Figure 4.1). Should they find that the sensory information is too much, they can close that channel and any residual sensory data will dissipate into the surrounding area.

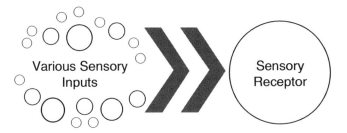

Figure 4.1 Neurotypical sensory perception

For those of us with Asperger syndrome, however, sensory information reaches us through a funnel that focuses and intensifies that information before it enters the sensory system (Figure 4.2). Because our sensory system is hypersensitive, it means that the brain is making it 'manageable' by effectively slowing it down. In the situation where there is too much sensory data coming in, the funnel becomes blocked by the data coming in. If the sensory input is terminated, rather than any residual data dissipating into the surrounding area, this is held in place by the walls of the funnel and hence continues to enter. The excess data will therefore only really stop affecting us after it has had the chance to be compressed into the funnel and finally into our sensory system. It is during this period of time that we cannot 'escape' from the effects of the excessive input that we tend to experience sensory overload. Effects of sensory overload differ per individual, but can include things such as headaches, panic attacks, inability to speak, inability to communicate, emotional outbursts and even the activation of co-morbid (or co-existing) conditions, such as epilepsy or asthma.

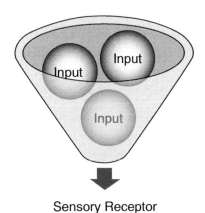

Sensory Receptor

Figure 4.2 Asperger sensory perception

Need for time alone

Frequently as a result of the sensory overload issues discussed, we often need periods of time alone to recuperate. Coping with overloads, or even just the 'business as usual' coping strategies, takes a lot of effort, and we require time apart from others to recover our energies. In a period of stress, this need for 'personal time' increases as it takes longer for us to recover.

Hypervigilance

It is not surprising that people who have hypersensitivities tend to experience hypervigilance. This is when we are acutely aware of our surroundings and constantly on a look-out for things that can be perceived as threats, especially when we have recently had an overload experience. For example, someone with visual hypersensitivity could have experienced a recent overload due to working in an office with a faulty overhead light. The next week at work, that same individual is likely to be overly tense and observant regarding anything to do with the lights or visual stimuli.

Loss of focus

I must say that I find it interesting to read about the concept of what is termed monotropism (Murrie, Lesser and Lawson 2005). Monotropism is where we pay attention to or perceive detail, but struggle with seeing the big picture or whole. Attwood (2007) refers to this as weak central coherence. My belief about leaders with Asperger syndrome is that we have been able to develop strategies to redress this shortcoming quite early in our school careers, and that we have quite adept central coherence by the time we start our careers. I would be the last to say that we do not still have the propensity to get stuck in the detail, as you would have seen from what I have been discussing in the book so far. However, I believe it to be an area we have of necessity worked hard to compensate for.

There is one example provided by Tony Attwood (2007), however, that I personally do not agree with. In discussing the subject of weak central coherence, Attwood describes our attention to detail as being similar to a person looking at the world through a rolled-up piece of paper, hence not seeing a lot of information. I dare to counter that example. I believe that actually we tend to see a lot more detail than most people. Far from seeing only a restricted view through the rolled-up paper, we see *everything*. Let me give you my own example for this. Imagine a situation where a family are sitting in their lounge. Suddenly they hear an unusual noise outside. In one scenario, the father asks his neurotypical son to have a look outside and tell them what he sees. The son goes to the window and feeds back that he sees nothing – he has perceived that everything looks normal. In the second scenario, the father asks his Asperger son to look outside and tell them what he sees. The son goes to the window and feeds back that he sees the following: it is sunny, there is a light breeze that is moving the leaves on the trees nearby, there is a squirrel on the pathway, there are a number of cumulus clouds developing, there is a small fly caught in a spider's web on the outside of the window, there is a pair of turtle doves on the bush nearby... We do not see part of the picture outside the window, we see *everything*. Where we have a challenge is actually determining what from that information is relevant and what isn't. In the above example, the neurotypical son had attuned to look for something out of the ordinary, and therefore filtered out anything irrelevant. The son with Asperger's was not able to do this effectively.

As we have grown, we have developed techniques to recognise what we need to focus on and what we need to ignore or put aside to process later. Unlike neurotypicals, we do not automatically filter information. It is something we need to learn to do. By the time we have reached high school, this is generally something we can do quite effectively in normal circumstances.

However, in situations of stress, we may find that we become more distracted by irrelevant information. In a way, we regress to a situation where we could be having a conversation with someone about a very important topic only to interrupt ourselves mid-sentence to comment on the colour of butterfly that just flew past, or the unusual hairstyle of a colleague passing by in the corridor outside the meeting room.

Shutdowns

Shutdowns can often occur as a result of sensory overload. As a means to cut out this overwhelming bombardment of information and sensory data, we teach ourselves to block out the world. We switch off or shut down. Sometimes we do this by totally ceasing to function, by going into our room and staring into space. However, for most of us, one of the ways we do this is to become totally engrossed in something. At work, this could mean that we sit down in front of our computer and effectively shut out the rest of the office. We don't hear, see or feel anything other than the computer. We are in a bubble.

In times of stress, we may find that we are starting to do this more frequently. We end up distancing ourselves from others unintentionally, and can be seen to be ignoring the people around us.

Perfectionism

Many of us experience a level of personal perfectionism in areas where we believe we can do well. Our thinking tends to be black or white, and therefore we tend to see our own performance as either good or bad. As people with Asperger syndrome, we tend to put a high value on the concept of intelligence (this is more fully discussed in Chapter 8). Generally, this is because we see it as an area where we are not hindered by any developmental disorders, and one we have not had to struggle with as much as other areas, such as social and communication skills. We obtain a lot of our sense of worth from our ability to perform well. Any perception on our part that we are underperforming can cause great frustration and stress for us.

So we have covered why it is important to understand how you react to change. Shall we examine the actual effects?

Order and routine

Almost everyone with Asperger syndrome craves order and routine. However, by the time we have become leaders within business, we have learnt to find ways to ensure that this predisposition does not become an undue focus for us. However, when a situation becomes stressful, we can revert to needing order and routine around us. We can end up spending significant amounts of time ordering our desks, or categorising projects, or developing a new labelling technique for our calendars. Similarly, we may develop an increased tendency to adhere rigidly to rules and established procedures during times of stress, far more than we ordinarily would.

Stimming

Stimming (abbreviated from the word stimulating) is where we undertake some kind of repetitive physical activity aimed at focusing our attention away from a stressor and therefore bringing that stress under control. Examples of stimming would include rapid finger tapping, rapid toe or foot tapping, rocking, humming, finger or hand flapping or bouncing in one's seat. As with most things, stimming is highly individual. For those of us who have been in business for a long time, we have either learnt to suppress any stimming, or to convert to a type of stimming which is more 'socially acceptable'. However, when a situation becomes stressful, it is highly likely that stimming may increase, or you may inadvertently revert to what you may consider your less favourable stimming methods.

Understanding the effects of change

The above are some of the main ways that stress can affect you as someone with Asperger syndrome. A change programme is going to introduce an element of insecurity for you, irrespective of how well prepared you are for it; hence you need to be aware of how the related stress will affect your functioning.

So in what ways can a change programme create insecurities for you? Some of the more obvious ways would include the following:

- the risk of redundancy/cost-cuts affecting your department or function
- the risk of redundancy/cost-cuts affecting your role in particular
- the risk of being unable to complete the project to the satisfaction of senior management
- the risk of running over budget
- the risk of over-running in terms of the project plan timescales
- the risk of losing important members of your team
- the risk of additional workloads.

In each one of the above scenarios, there is a very obvious element of insecurity. Who would not feel insecure if they knew there was the potential for headcount cuts in their department, or that they could be expected to perform according to some new and potentially challenging performance standards?

But what about the sort of change programme where there is no formally identified risk for you as leader of the programme? Let's consider some scenarios where this may apply.

Scenario 1: Promotion as part of restructuring

Jenny Hawkins is one of three Shared Service Centre Managers within a large call-centre. She has held the position now for three years, ever since the function was started. She was involved in the development of the centre and in defining the role of the centre in the ongoing strategy of the company.

At this year's strategic planning meeting, a decision was made by the Board of Directors to upgrade the Shared Services function, since it was becoming a key strategic focus for the business. As a result, it was decided that the function would be restructured and a Head of Shared Services would be appointed. Following a review of performance and an internal assessment programme, Jenny is offered the position, with her own role being filled by a member of her team.

Jenny is incredibly pleased with this achievement, since it is something that she had been speaking about informally with her own manager for quite some time. She had always felt that the function needed to be made more focal for the business, and now it seemed that her opinion had been taken seriously.

Feeling confident and motivated, Jenny made her way into the office on the first day following the announcement. She immediately went to her previous colleagues in the call-centre, the two other Shared Service Centre Managers, Julia and Patrick. She was excited and wanted to share her thoughts about the way forward with them. She started to have an informal chat with them, but immediately felt a difference in the atmosphere. She realised that these previous colleagues were now her direct subordinates, and that perhaps her informal banter was inappropriate, but she still thought of them as her friends. They seemed to be in the midst of a similar dilemma.

Leaving the call-centre, she made her way to the management office, where her new office had been prepared over the weekend. She wasn't used to working away from the call-centre shop-floor, but this was something that she was looking forward to.

Jenny's old manager was there waiting for her when she arrived, and advised her that she would now be reporting directly to the Finance Director, and that they would now be colleagues at the same level. There were a lot of new management policies and procedures which she needed to familiarise herself with, and she realised that she would need to learn the senior management culture and protocols within the company.

Arriving home from work that first day, Jenny was greeted by her partner.

'So, new Boss-Lady, did you have a brilliant first day?'

Jenny paused before answering, realising that her first day had not been as stress-free as she thought it would be. So many things were changing. Would she be able to cope?

So what can we tell from Scenario 1? Jenny Hawkins was someone who – if I had asked her whether she foresaw any cause for insecurity in her promotion – would have confidently said no. And yet, by the end of the first day, there were a number of insecurities niggling at the back of her head.

Let us look at a couple more scenarios where insecurities arose that were not anticipated beforehand.

Scenario 2: Upgrade of systems

Henry Walston had been campaigning for an upgrade to the company's management information system for what seemed like an eternity. The truth was that the current system being used by the organisation was not only out of date – it was archaic! Everyday statistics and figures which should flow seamlessly from a sophisticated IT system were, instead, manually pulled together after a download from what was little more than a glorified database.

He wasn't the only person who recognised this. Almost every manager in the company was up in arms about the lack of management information, and recognised that – as Management Information System Manager – Henry's hands were tied by the lack of adequate information technology.

And then it happened. The company had its external audit just prior to putting itself forward as an investor in people. Charles Davies, the Chief Executive, had proudly led the initiative and made sure that there was an adequate budget for PR covering what he thought would be an outstanding report on the higher than average performance of his organisation. What came back was a rather shocking report on the shortcomings of the company's reporting, largely linked to its use of redundant management information systems.

So within a week Henry had his approval to upgrade the MI system to whatever he felt was appropriate – and to do it as soon as possible. Henry had already been proactive in respect of the new system as part of his earlier motivation for an upgrade. He had taken time to meet with each of the Executive Committee to see what they felt the company needed from their MI system, and had also met with each head of department to ask the same question. He had communicated with all of them in respect of the new software to be installed, and had explained that the system would take a month to install and integrate. Henry was confident that the changes to be introduced by the new system were being introduced correctly, communicated well and – most of all – welcomed by all the managers in the company.

It was in week two that some of the problems began. Despite Henry communicating regularly with the management of the company regarding the time necessary for installation, a number of managers still came to members of his team demanding management information. He was able to calm them down by manually doing some reports for them, but this ended up creating additional problems in that those managers who had not complained got to hear about the 'special treatment' of some managers, and began to accuse Henry of 'playing favourites'.

Later, he discovered that there were problems developing internally within his department as well, since certain members of the team were struggling to understand the new system and were becoming stressed.

One day Henry was called through to have a meeting with the CEO. In the meeting Charles Davies shared his concerns about the way the implementation of the new system was being handled, and the complaints he had received from a few managers in respect of his providing information for some managers and not others. Although he appeared to be satisfied with Henry's responses in respect of both the implementation challenges and the misunderstanding about reports, Henry left the meeting feeling highly insecure about a change programme he never thought would represent a problem for him.

Scenario 3: SME with great response to advertisement

Build and Grow Limited was a start-up company started by entrepreneurs Jill and Geoffrey Menendes. The Menendes had both held senior roles within the financial services sector before deciding to start their own business advising small businesses wanting to invest.

It was decided at their fifth board meeting that it was time to place an advertisement in one of the leading investment magazines in order to get some more clients. They were mature enough now as a company to take on the increased workload, and they had invested in and trained new staff.

The week after the ad was in, the phone calls started to come through. The response to the advertisement was incredible, and the Menendes were exuberant. Within less than a month they had won an additional 12 contracts.

In the fourth week after the ad, however, things began to change. The response to the ad continued at the same high levels, and the number of clients on their books tripled. They soon realised that they had reached capacity in respect of dealing with new clients. Jill felt that they should be telling prospective clients that they could not take them on board at present, but promise to contact them as soon as they had capacity. Geoffrey felt that placing potential clients on a 'waiting list' would be seen as incredibly unprofessional, and would lose them more than just clients. They spoke about the potential for recruiting additional staff and realised that – although this could be a partial solution – this would require them to neglect their clients in order to train the new staff.

The subject of the next board meeting was obvious. How could something so positive end up being something potentially so negative?

Each of the above scenarios provides a different perspective on a potential insecurity for the individual or individuals concerned. Something that could possibly have been seen as being nothing other than a positive change will inevitably create some form of insecurity for everyone concerned – including you. It is important that you recognise that insecurity will be there during the period of change, and by recognising this you will be taking the first step towards coping with it.

Change involves discarding the past to move to the future

Again, this may appear to be an obvious comment, but so often this is far more complex for Asperger leaders than we realise. As described in the following chapter when we elaborate on the employees, what this actually amounts to is a type of loss of one sort or another.

When we say that we need to discard the past in order to move to the future, we do tend to think of this in terms of systems and processes. So we will no longer be making use of the old software system, or we will no longer follow policy X but now policy Y. It is fair to say that this certainly does constitute part of what we mean by discarding the past. However, you need to realise that this is only a small part of what needs to be left behind.

Some of the more challenging tasks a leader in a business needs to address include the following:

- discarding current working relationships – both up and down

- discarding the working practices you have set up for your department/team for business-as-usual processes

- discarding routine in favour of the initial disorder of change

- discarding key elements of the psychological contract with your team in such areas as, for example, job security, role security and a stress-free working environment

- discarding current customs and culture in favour of the new one to be introduced or developed

- making sure people around you 'walk the talk'

- making sure *you* 'walk the talk'.

In short, there is no way that the business will be able to move forward to the new situation until such time as a definitive line has been drawn under the old way of doing things. This is not always easy – especially for those of us with Asperger syndrome who have been with the company for a while and have played a key role in developing those systems, relationships and customs we are now about to discard! Because many of these leadership tasks are areas we have had to put a lot of additional effort into in order to be successful, this has given us a greater sense of ownership of these areas. Giving up on them, therefore, can be extremely difficult.

Many people in a change situation become extremely stressed because they are experiencing a 'niggling feeling of discomfort', as one of my clients so aptly put it. They attribute this to an impending problem, or some kind of intuitive sense that something is wrong or about to go wrong. Recognising the fact that this sense of discomfort is largely the result of inherent insecurity or loss of the familiar will – very often – help to alleviate those feelings.

But there are other, less obvious, ways in which a change programme will affect you. One of the most common involves the way that you manage your business as usual. Management styles in a change environment need to change quite significantly. You are no longer focusing on maintaining a stable, consistent 'business as usual' department. Instead, your team needs to fit business as usual into a programme of change such that neither one is neglected as a result of the other. Consequently, subordinates may feel challenged and find that their previous relationship with you as manager has either changed or is being stretched.

Business skills are likely to be tested in new areas as well. Change programmes require project management skills, financial skills, strategic skills. For some managers, this simply has not been an area where they have been required to have skills to date. For them, the change programme can become stressful.

Perhaps the most important area that needs to be recognised as an area where change will affect you is in the area of people management. As already mentioned, your leadership style will need to be adapted to one more appropriate to a change situation. Not only that, but you will be required to help your team work through the same effects of change that you have just identified for yourself, potentially at a more intensive level. You will need to lead them through the change, and ensure both that business as usual is happening and that the team is moving in the direction of required change with the correct attitude and mind-set, and that they are not going to jump ship due to the stresses created.

The way that change is managed and communicated can make the difference between the acceptance or rejection of the changes by the people in the organisation. We will cover this topic in more detail later in the book. But the point I make here is that this management and communication of change lies at the feet of the people managers in the organisation – at every level. This is a significant increase in the level of people skills, and this in itself can create additional pressures for managers or leaders who are not used to such a highly intensive people strategy. For those of us with Asperger syndrome, it can put a strain on a competence we have been able to 'get by' with up until now, but which is now going to move to the next level. The remainder of this book is intended to assist you with this particular challenge. Once again, however, recognising that this could be an area of stress for you will ultimately help you cope.

Dealing with ambiguity

One recommendation I make to you as you prepare yourself for the change programme is this. Change is a period of significant ambiguity in most cases, and this ambiguity can cause many strong leaders finally to snap and give in to the pressures of the unknown.

During many types of change programme, such as during a merger, an acquisition or a downsizing exercise, there are going to be times when the information flow from the top down is going to seem to stop. This is a necessary part of the process. At times information just cannot be filtered down; at other times the information updates are just not there.

However, as a leader of change, you are required to reassure the people who report to you in respect of just such ambiguities, and therein lies the challenge. You may be feeling that the ambiguity is extremely difficult to deal with, but you cannot allow that emotion to become visible to your team. You need to be the one who shows that the change is achievable, that the ambiguity is something that can be tolerated and overcome.

If you allow your team to know that ambiguity is making you uncomfortable, it will create even greater levels of insecurity amongst them, and their levels of resistance – whether active or passive – will grow.

The greatest strength you will have as a leader of change is the strength to reflect confidence and assurance despite inner turmoil. Very often this does not come naturally, and people do need to take some time to build this into their day-to-day way of working. If you have the time, invest some of your personal time in thinking about how you are going to deal with the uncertainties and ambiguities that may arise during your project, and how that will impact on other people.

Chapter 13 will provide some more insight into how you can prepare yourself for the change to come.

Chapter 5

Understanding How Change Affects *Them*

In much the same way as applies to yourself, in order to best deal with some of the effects of change on the people around you it is necessary to first understand what those effects are likely to be.

We discussed the psychological contract in Chapter 2, where we made mention of the possible negative effects of a change in this contract. Let us look now at this in a bit more detail.

What are some of the key elements of the unwritten psychological contract that can either be broken or tested during a change programme? One of the more obvious ones is that of *job security*. Most change programmes initiated as a result of restructuring, mergers or performance management contain the inevitable cost-containment requirements. In many cases, this will include a direct reference to headcount in the organisation.

People who are being advised of a major change programme are, more often than not, fully aware of the fact that change often spells redundancies. If, on the other hand, they are fortunate enough to have been so shielded from the change programmes of the last couple of decades that they are not aware of the potential consequence, they will certainly hear about the potential for redundancies from colleagues or associates who *have* been in contact with it very quickly.

Another element that can be affected is that of *role security*. Whilst an employee may be told that there will be no redundancies, how will the change affect their role? Will the nature of the role change? Will the reporting lines change? Will the autonomy levels increase/decrease?

A related element is that of *career security*. Most people want to progress within the organisation they join. They plan to be promoted as they grow within the company, and to be given the opportunity to develop their careers. However, if a significant change programme is initiated, people will begin to wonder about the ongoing potential for their careers. Will this change put a ceiling on their progression in the organisation? Will the change negatively affect their curriculum vitae, if they are professional people? Will the change add another five years to their progression towards a management position?

We know that Asperger leaders have a tendency more easily to overlook the social side of the employment contract. People tend to build strong relationships in the workplace. Unlike most of us with Asperger syndrome, neurotypical employees generally feel that this is central to their working experience, and changes to social relationships are considered a significant challenge to the ongoing experience of a workplace. Employee satisfaction surveys are tools used by the human resources departments of organisations to try to determine how people perceive their experience of working at the company. Its main objectives are to identify areas that are perceived as unsatisfactory for the enjoyment of the work experience, and those that contribute towards a positive work experience, and to provide employees the opportunity to raise any concerns that they have. In surveys I have run for clients, two elements of the work experience almost always indicated within the top three keys to a positive work experience are positive relationships with colleagues and a good relationship with their line manager. In other words, two critically important keys to a positive work experience, from the employees' perspective, are socially related.

A change programme has the potential to disrupt social relationships significantly within the organisation, or at least in parts of it, either through one or other of the parties being made redundant, having to move offices, being promoted, getting a new role, and so on.

People also tend to be very suspicious of changes in an organisation – why have the directors initiated a change programme? Is the company in trouble? Are they trying to get more money for themselves? Is the company doing so well it is going to be sold or split? The rumour mill is a very powerful and disruptive force in the workplace, and I will cover this very important topic in Chapter 19.

Neurotypical behaviours associated with the phases of the psychological change cycle

In Chapter 3 we went into the detail of the stages of the transition process and the related phases of the psychological change cycle. We are now going to build on that description to make it useful for us. We need to be able to recognise what sorts of *behaviours* are associated with these phases and identify those that are inappropriate or have the potential to cause a problem in order that we can be proactive in taking any action. Let us detail the sorts of behaviours that tend to manifest within the different phases of the psychological change cycle and then consider how to recognise them.

Let me start this section by clarifying my terminology. In many cases I am going to be referring to the way neurotypicals react or behave in certain circumstances. This is not to stay that those of us with Asperger syndrome will not experience these sorts of reactions. However, the focus here is on how neurotypical individuals will generally act.

Transitional Stage 1: Introversion
PHASE 1: SHOCK/NUMBNESS

People experiencing shock tend to describe this as 'overwhelming' or 'mind-numbing'. I think the latter phrase is probably the most appropriate for this phase. Neurotypical individuals will have an experience that – to be fair – most of us with Asperger syndrome are quite familiar with. This is the experience of 'brain-freeze'. Whereas we tend to experience this as a result of sensory overload, for neurotypical individuals this can occur as the result of shock. It is the neurotypical's own form of sensory overload! It is possibly, therefore, the one phase that we can best understand as far as behaviours go. People will go silent, be non-responsive or struggle to respond, and frequently appear to be 'in a daze'. The person will appear distracted or 'somewhere else'. Without a doubt, productivity will suffer due to a lack of concentration.

PHASE 2: DENIAL

Behaviours associated with denial include being flippant or overly casual about the situation, and possibly undermining it or ridiculing it. As already mentioned, typical comments during this phase would be 'That doesn't apply to me', 'It won't affect my role' or 'They're just talking about it – it won't really happen.' However, just because a person doesn't verbalise in a way that indicates they are in denial does not exclude them from experiencing it. Some people will just become extremely focused on continuing to work exactly as they always have. Ironically, work productivity actually tends to improve during this phase, as people in denial focus on getting things done the way they have always been done, and doing it in such a way as to show that there is no need to change things.

PHASE 3: DEFENSIVE BLAMING

Once people have reached Phase 3 of the change cycle, they have started to experience frustration and anger at the fact that the situation is changing and they are not in control. People can become short-tempered with colleagues, lose patience with subordinates or become insubordinate towards their managers. Work often suffers, as individuals struggle to concentrate, and find fault with everything. This is the stage of 'nit-picking' (where neurotypicals tend to make a big deal of even small errors) and 'finger-pointing' (where neurotypicals try to place the blame for all problems on other people, making sure that they are not associated with any failures or shortcomings). People will also start to get angry with themselves, often chastising themselves for not seeing things coming, or not making sure they did enough beforehand to make change unnecessary. The key neurotypical response at this time is anger. Outbursts and shortness from a person who normally works well with others is a very likely signal that the individual is in Phase 3.

PHASE 4: PANIC/DREAD

At this time, the individual's anger starts to be replaced by worry and dread. They realise that this change is going to affect them, that their work is likely to be under scrutiny, that their job might be at risk. Errors can start to appear in work, or the person could start to take longer than usual on their work, trying to ensure that no errors fall through the gaps. Communication suffers as the neurotypical starts spending their time worrying about themselves rather than thinking about talking to others. Ill health may start to be an issue as stress levels build. People could start working longer than they usually do, or they could start having problems with timekeeping.

PHASE 5: DEPRESSION AND INSECURITY

The phase of depression and insecurity is also probably an area into which we as Asperger leaders may have some insight. Depression can cripple an individual by causing them to disconnect from others in the workplace, lose motivation to come to work and lose the ability to think coherently or to be productive. Neurotypicals in this phase tend to shut themselves off from others and function at their lowest levels. Productivity suffers and morale can be brought down in those working with them.

Transitional Stage 2: Analysis
PHASE 6: CONTEMPLATION

Central to the contemplation phase is that people start to communicate again. Individuals appear to be starting to take notice of what is going on around them in the workplace, and start to ask questions. Many describe it as 'coming out of a box'. Energy levels start to rise and productivity tends to improve. Individuals start talking about the present and the future, not the past.

PHASE 7: ACKNOWLEDGEMENT

In this phase, people have acknowledged that the change is happening, and their behaviours reflect this. They will be starting to direct their actions in line with the changes taking place, continuing to ask questions about the future, and also making positive contributions towards the change process. Commitment to taking the situation seriously is there, and individuals will want more than ever to have as much information as possible about what is happening and about their role in the new vision.

Transitional Stage 3: Acceptance and testing
PHASE 8: EXPERIMENTATION

In the experimentation phase, individuals are beginning to take those first positive steps to see if this is going to work for them. They are starting to see the way, and are likely to be proactively asking questions and also making suggestions. Employees begin to try out new behaviours, or undertake project work to formalise the change. When there is a formal change programme in place, this is where the project teams start working in earnest. Generally this is a phase with a great deal of energy as a result of the activity, and this energy needs to be channelled correctly to avoid misunderstanding or frustration between members of the team – and between members of the team and those on the outside.

PHASE 9: DISCOVERY/LEARNING

As individuals apply themselves to the change process, they start to become encouraged by the new elements of their work, the new challenges and new ideas. Generally, this acts as a motivation to continue with the change, although for some people this may be a challenge if they do not handle learning new processes, methods or situations very well. In many cases, this will apply to many of us, as people with Asperger's.

PHASE 10: REFLECTION

Reflection is the first step towards internalising the new situation, or starting to withdraw from it – it is the process of personalising it apart from the very strong emotions experienced in Stages 1–3. During this phase, individuals will start to turn inward again, but with a less negative focus. They are likely to start asking additional questions about how they can be involved in the future, the impact they are making in the present as well as making some suggestions as to how they may prefer things to go. The focus is forward, not backwards.

As mentioned in Chapter 3, Transitional Stage 4 consists of two routes, although an individual can move between the two routes as time goes on. To simplify the analysis, I present these as two separate routes.

Transitional Stage 4: Route 1 – Resolution
PHASE 11: OPTIMISM

The individual finds that they are becoming optimistic and enthusiastic about their new situation. They become more social and relaxed, and will tend to laugh and joke more. They also tend to be able to discuss parts of the change process that were previously considered too difficult to face due to the negative feelings attached. Very often this is a time when people will start becoming more creative and productive.

PHASE 12: SATISFACTION

Feeling satisfied with the changes, their role in it and their place in the organisation post-change, the individual will become far more forward-looking and ambitious within the company. The outlook changes from 'If this change is successful…' to 'Now that this has been successful…'

PHASE 13: INTEGRATION

Having integrated into the new environment and accepted the post-change environment as their current and future situation, any losses associated with the past are forgotten or overcome. The person will tend to revert to the same normal behaviours they had before the changes, and sometimes their attitudes, productivity and involvement may even improve. If they have been involved with the change process, this will provide them with a sense of ownership and inclusion that creates a very strong association with the organisation and others in it.

Transitional Stage 4: Route 2 – Regression
PHASE 11: UNCERTAINTY

Signals that an individual is starting to move towards a Route 2 path during the fourth stage of the transition is that they will start to withdraw from activities they were previously a part of. Socially, they may start to be less open. Within the business, they may start holding back in meetings, or make negative comments. A common expression at this time is 'I don't understand why…'

PHASE 12: DISSATISFACTION

The individual becomes more and more dissatisfied with the status quo and frequently starts reverting to previous behaviours or thought patterns. They may start raising previous work methods in meetings, or handing in work that reflects use of processes no longer in effect. Phrases often used at this time include 'when it was done properly', 'before things got messed up' and 'when people knew what they were doing'.

Alternatively, people may start talking about the way things should be or could be, even though the changes have already taken place.

PHASE 13: WITHDRAWAL

Here the person has decided (consciously or subconsciously) that they do not fit within the new environment and withdraw, either purely mentally or both physically and mentally through resignation. If they remain in the organisation, they tend to revert to previous ways of working, or stop performing any of the new activities they have been undertaking since the change, potentially subconsciously sabotaging new systems and processes. It is difficult for them to work as a team with other people, since they often appear difficult or confrontational, or set in their ways. People will either avoid them, or they will make other people who are currently on Route 1 sway into Route 2 due to uncertainty caused.

Understanding the impact of change

In trying to understand what people in the company will be going through psychologically as a result of a change programme, there are seven main constructs you need to be aware of.

1. *Change always creates insecurity* – All of the behaviours discussed above are very real elements of the insecurities people face when change happens in the workplace. No matter what type of change is being introduced, or how well you think it is going to be received, insecurities will arise. We have already discussed how insecurity will affect the leader of change in general. The same principles apply to those people who are generally even more directly affected by the change.

   One element of the change process that will have a strong effect on reinforcing insecurity is that of ambiguity. For individuals who do not have a direct input into the change decisions, this element can create significant concerns. After all, people will find themselves in a situation where specific information in respect of outcomes – or even processes – surrounding the change is just not available. This topic will be covered in more detail in Chapter 14.

2. *People have an inherent need for stability and security* – Once again, this may seem like an obvious statement, and yet so many times senior management overlooks this when communicating change. Identified as a core requirement for us as individuals (Schön 1971), the sudden loss of stability and security in our work lives will overflow into our personal lives, leaving us feeling stressed and usually angry (key elements of Phase 3 of the psychological change cycle). This ultimately leads to resistance to change, and an attempt to go back to the way things were.

3. *Change involves loss in one form or another* – The above may seem like quite a strong statement, and yet it is very pertinent here. Discussing the psychological contract should have given you an understanding of how important certain elements of the employment relationship are to individuals, especially neurotypicals. When these are taken away, their absence is treated as a loss. But the elements lost do not have to be tangible or even visible things. For example, job security is not something that you are going to be able to see – it is intrinsic, and the value to the individual is very personal and unique. The loss of this intrinsic motivator can be an incredible psychological shock for an individual, particularly if they were not properly prepared for the loss or if it is the first time they have had to face any job insecurity.

4. *Change is treated either as an opportunity or as a threat* – There are generally two reactions to an announcement of change: seeing the change as an opportunity or seeing the change as a threat. Perceptions of opportunity will lead the individual to be open to what is coming, despite any insecurities, and to work with the leadership team to achieve what is seen as a better state. Perceptions of the change as a threat will result in the individual becoming defensive, withdrawing rather than participating in the change programme, showing passive resistance or inactivity, and potentially becoming rebellious or disruptive. Whatever extrinsic form their perception of threat takes, you can be assured that it will be negative.

5. *Change leads to a focus on self* – Even if an employee sees the change as a potential opportunity, an unavoidable side-effect of change – whether this is conscious or subconscious – is that the employee will start to show

self-protective behaviour. This is part of the first stage of transition in the psychological change cycle, discussed in Chapter 3. What do we mean by this? People will start to think about their own position in the company, their own significance, their own continued security in the corporate family. For some people this will result in an active defence in the form of aggressively promoting themselves, or undermining others around them, and by trying to leverage themselves into strategic positions. Others may do this by keeping out of the line of fire and making sure that they are in the right place at the right time.

6. *Change leads to frustration* – Change for an individual will always lead to frustration, although the extent and duration of this can vary considerably. Frustration as a result of a perception of change as a threat is easily understandable, but managers are often surprised when they realise that even those who see the change as an opportunity are experiencing some type of frustration. This can vary from the frustration of anticipation, to the frustration of lowered expectations in respect of a positive change, or even just the frustration of insecurity whilst the changes are taking place.

7. *In the absence of guidance, people find a target for their frustration* – As mentioned, all people going through change will experience frustration of one sort or another during the process. An outlet for this frustration will be sought by default as a coping mechanism, and this is something that managers need to be very aware of. Depending on the nature of relationships, this can result in targeting against the manager, colleagues in the department, senior management, or the identified change agent within the company (such as a change management consultant). Such targeting will have the effect of undermining change efforts and could seriously derail your project and can very well be the main source of a rumour mill in the company.

As a practical exercise in considering how the psychological change cycle affects individuals, what follows is a hypothetical case study of two human resources managers going through a change programme. The different phases of the psychological change cycle have been indicated here, from each participant's perspective, to give you a better idea of their separate journeys.

Case study: Merger announcement at Corpus

Jack Hancroft and Susie Gibson made their way up to the presentation room on the fifth floor, chatting comfortably as they went. Both Jack and Susie were Human Resources Managers at Corpus Services Ltd, a well-established actuarial firm in the City.

'So, Jack, any idea what this meeting is about?' Susie asked as they entered the room.

'Not a clue. All I know is that it was called rather suddenly, and most of the staff are here, as well as HR as a whole.'

Tim Beresford, Human Resources Director for Corpus, Glenda Samuels, Chief Operating Officer, and Andrew Levine, CEO, were in the presentation room when the two HR colleagues entered. They exchanged a quick glance, surprised at the apparent 'heavy-weights' giving the presentation. After a few moments, Tim opened the meeting.

Half an hour later people started to leave the presentation hall. Jack and Susie walked together in silence. Neither one of them seemed able to do anything other than walk automatically towards their offices. [*Numbness*] Eventually Susie stopped and put her hand on Jack's arm.

'This is scary, Jack. I've never been in a merger situation before. What will that mean for the HR department? Is it going to affect our roles? What about our employment contacts?' [*Panic/dread*]

Jack frowned at Susie and shook his head.

'Oh, don't be so dramatic, Susie. Nothing's going to change. So we are involved with some kind of business transaction with another company. It doesn't mean we're going through some sort of restructuring!' [*Denial*]

Susie stared at Jack in disbelief.

'But of course it does, Jack! They *said* so – why do you think they called the meeting! This has obviously been going on for ages – we're only just finding out now. I can't believe I didn't recognise the signs.' [*Defensive blaming*]

Jack tutted his irritation at Susie's obvious display of emotion, and made his way to his office.

Susie walked slowly to her own office and opened up her email system. After an hour of answering urgent correspondence, she sat back and turned to face the window. Some of the emails that had been coming through to her over the last couple of weeks now started to make a bit more sense. Requests for management information – salary data, headcount and turnover stats – it just made sense now.

She sighed and rubbed her temples. Thinking about it, she knew that the company had been talking about diversifying into the corporate finance arena as opposed to purely risk. There certainly was an opportunity to grow the company significantly if this merger took place. And there would certainly be greater opportunities to develop her HR experience in respect of M&A work. [*Contemplation*] Obviously, it was going to happen – it was the logical thing for the company to do... [*Acknowledgement*]

Jack sat silently in his office after everyone had gone home for the evening. Reaching across, he switched off the overhead light, allowing the darkness to surround him – the only light coming from the computer screen in front of him.

Who did they think they were? He had been working here for ten whole years, and *this* is how they let him find out about some stupid merger programme? Had they deliberately kept the information from him? Did they think he was a FOOL?!? [*Defensive blaming*]

Jack jumped to his feet and began marching backwards and forwards across his office floor. One more year. That was all he needed. One more year! Then he would have been in line for the position of Assistant HR Director. But no. Nooooo. Now they have to start some stupid merger discussions which could destroy any chance of his promotion.

Jack stopped abruptly. Promotion? What was he thinking about promotion for? What was to say they hadn't already earmarked him for redundancy? After all, surely if they felt he was a worthwhile asset within the company they would have brought him in on the merger discussions before announcing it to the others. After all, he was the most senior HR person other than Tim Beresford. And Susie. Yes... Susie... [*Panic/dread*]

Tim Beresford was busy tackling a rather complicated spreadsheet when Susie came to see him. It had been a week since the announcement to the staff of the merger plans, and the reaction had been mixed. However, it was fair to say that the majority of the organisation had taken the news really negatively.

Tim looked up with a strained smile.

'Susie. What can I do for you?'

Susie paused a moment as she looked at her boss, the stress already apparent on his face. For the first time since the announcement she felt a touch of sympathy for him. She smiled.

'The question is, Tim, what can I do for you?'

Quickly she moved round the table and laid before the HR Director a short document and project plan.

'I've been thinking about the situation at Corpus. The announcement really seems to have caused some negative feelings out there, and the fact that management doesn't appear to be doing anything at the moment is making things worse. So I thought I would do a little homework in respect of the proposed change. This a draft communication plan and an outline project plan for the employee relations side of the merger. I haven't addressed any of the other areas – they aren't really my forte – but I thought that this may help us in getting the ball rolling on the employee comms side?' [*Experimentation/optimism*]

Tim glanced through the documents placed before him before looking up at his subordinate.

'Susie, I knew I could count on you.'

It had taken a while for Jack to come to terms with this new situation. He really wasn't one for change, and didn't really like to spend a lot of time talking about it. This change had been forced on him and he had to accept it whether he liked it or not. [*Contemplation*] So Susie had gone and made a name for herself by pulling together some silly project plans and communication plans – well, okay, perhaps the communication plans weren't bad – but now he had to start taking accountability for those areas of the project plan which had been assigned to him. [*Learning*] Although he had to say that he found Susie's enthusiasm a bit over the top. If only she would just come back down to earth and see the huge hassle this all represented. [*Dissatisfaction*] Well, at least there were only three weeks of the project left before life could start getting back to something more normal – whatever that might be! [*Withdrawal*]

Susie sat before Tim in her annual performance review meeting, discussing the recent merger activity and her role in it. Tim had encouraged her to talk about how the change had affected her and some of the lessons she had learnt as part of the process, and this encouraged her to think about her experience in a lot more detail than she had. [*Reflection*]

'I suppose,' she said, 'the one thing that I didn't actually realise before this was just how much duplication of work was going on in our area. Until we started looking at who was doing exactly what, and what our resources were, I had no idea that we had five administrators doing exactly the same job when we only needed two. I suppose it has helped me to re-examine my role in the light of a more centralised approach to HR. I had never really done that. I also found that the amount of communication and counselling I had to do with the staff as a whole gave me such a deeper understanding of the importance of communication in this process. Yes, I did have some challenges with some of my colleagues who were struggling with the changes, but I think that I coped well and developed some people skills in the process. It certainly improved my project management skills as well. All in all, I think I gained an incredible amount of insight into the way the future organisation should be operating, and my role in helping us to reach that state.' [*Satisfaction*]

Susie finished her review meeting feeling satisfied and fulfilled. Despite the upheaval, it had been a good year, and the change that had been introduced had made such a difference to performance. She continued thinking about her progress over the last year as she logged into the new HR Information System and automatically pulled down a web-publishing element which would send her report directly to the management intranet. Although this was a new system and a new way of operating within HR, Susie undertook the task automatically, her mind still focused on the positives of her last year with the company. [*Integration*]

Jack sat in the interview room of National Merchandising Ltd, speaking to the Recruiting Manager.

'So what was your main reason for leaving Corpus, Mr Hancroft?'

'Mainly because of the changes going on in the company. We went through a merger with another company, and the systems which they wanted us to implement were far, far ahead of where we actually were at the time. I mean, it really was a case of trying to change too much too soon. I must admit that I often had to go back to the old systems just to get things done, which wasn't very productive. [*Regression*] Eventually, I just felt that I couldn't see the logic of where Corpus was trying to get to, or at least how they thought they could possibly get where they wanted to be and still retain their key staff. [*Reflection*]

'I've worked with them for over ten years – I know the way they think. This change programme was just too much of a change for them.' [*Withdrawal*]

Reading through the above hypothetical case study should highlight one important consideration in respect of the phases of the psychological change cycle, namely that not every phase may be experienced by each individual. For example, Susie went from numbness straight to panic, whereas Jack never experienced contemplation or acceptance. In fact, it is highly likely that the reason Jack ultimately regressed was that he never did go through those two important phases of contemplation and acceptance. After all, if you can never accept the changes going on around you as being valid or of value to you personally, there is no way that you can internalise them.

As we continue our discussion of change and how this will affect both yourself and your people, the above phases of the psychological change cycle may be referred to either implicitly or explicitly. For no matter how much we may want to make a change exercise a purely logical, rational or systematic operation – an approach that does tend to appeal to us as leaders with Asperger syndrome – change involves people with emotions and personalities that are unique and unpredictable – often, even to themselves!

Forlaron stated that the importance of the human side of change should never be underestimated, and that consideration be given to causes of potential resistance, as well as what sort of motivators are built into the processes going forward (Forlaron 2005). In developing your change programme, therefore, make sure that this development is tempered with a strong dose of human empathy, or the best-laid project plan could ultimately fail.

Taking the above constructs into consideration, it can be readily seen that the human factor in a change programme is quite a key one. You will need to ensure that you, as someone with Asperger syndrome who is leading a change programme, are prepared for the emotional shake-up which generally accompanies the announcement (or rumour!) of change. Not taking into account how the programme will influence the people you lead and the resultant side-effects of their reactions is something you need to ensure you avoid.

Exercise 1 in Part 4 of the book provides you with the opportunity to apply some of the information you have been reading to your own experience of change. I recommend that you undertake this exercise before continuing.

Chapter 6

Understanding How Change Affects the Organisation

In understanding change and how it affects us, it is critically important that we acknowledge the overall effect that change can have on the organisation as a whole. Whilst we have already discussed the effects of change on both yourself and other individuals in the company, this chapter deals with the effect of change on the collective whole of the organisation – as evidenced through the organisational culture. Organisational cultures and the 'unspoken laws' people in organisations adhere to can differ significantly, and this can tangibly alter the potential for success of a change programme. In order for us to understand and lead change in our organisations, we need to understand the organisational 'animal' such that it is, and how we can affect it by the changes we introduce.

All organisations – be they small, national or multinational – can be thought of as complex systems, and there are a number of organisational development models that have been used over the years to assist in understanding that complexity. I do not intend to elaborate on this within this book, since it is not the focus of our discussion. Suffice to say that organisations have been compared to machines, brains, organisms, cultures and political systems, to name a few (Morgan 1997). As a person with Asperger syndrome, I tend to identify with those comparisons which are more process-driven, such as the machine and brain comparisons. However, I also recognise that this tends to be because I used to think about organisations systematically, rather than taking into account the human element. I believe that organisations should be considered almost living, breathing creatures that can change their behaviours in response to rewards, punishments, fear, excitement and change. That may sound strange for someone reading this for the first time, never having really considered the organisation to be anything other than an institution, building or entity. However, try to reconcile this with the understanding that the organisation – as we are discussing it – is actually no more than the combined whole of a whole range of individuals, with individual behaviours and reactions to change.

By considering the organisations in this way, we are considering the company in terms of group dynamics – how groups of people interact, influence each other and become a unified (or sometimes disparate) whole.

Understandably there are a number of effects that change will have on the organisation, both positive and negative. The purpose of this chapter, however, is to highlight some of the negative effects on the organisation which are a result of employees' reactions to change. This should help you recognise when a change programme is having detrimental effects, allowing you time to correct and reverse those effects.

Let us examine some of the more disruptive effects of negative responses to change in the organisation in more detail.

Individualism increases and team play decreases

As discussed previously, one effect of change for the individual is an increased focus on self and self-preservation. As a result of people beginning to feel insecure and uncertain of their futures, they are going to start looking inward at their own opportunities for survival within the changing corporate environment.

Suddenly the team motto of 'All for one and one for all' doesn't seem so important any more. Instead, what matters is whether their own individual needs and desires are going to be fulfilled in the future. In some of the more negative situations, people actively start to work against the team by undermining or challenging others in the team, with the hope that this will make the other person's role more vulnerable than their own.

This change in behaviour stems from a loss of trust – in the organisation, in the manager, in the senior leadership of the company. Who has caused the loss of trust is not really important; the results are the same. Teamwork suffers and 'office politics' come to the fore where they never have been highly visible in the past. In fact, where teamwork begins to suffer due to individual insecurities and hidden agendas, the office politics can become so intense that they can become a powerful stress factor in the workplace.

In order to ensure that the negative effects of individual insecurity do not affect the working of the team, it is very important that the change process includes a specific focus on the team and how it is working together. This is covered in Chapter 18 when we talk about providing opportunities for the team.

Power struggles start to affect work

Once again, individual insecurities can cause people to start to try to 'prove' their worth in the organisation, in order to ensure that they have a key role going forward. Especially in the case of change programmes such as mergers, acquisitions, downsizing and restructuring, where headcount is likely to be affected, most people begin to fight for what they see as theirs. As emphasised before, this can be either active or passive, but the point being made in this chapter is that the way people work starts to change.

Instead of working as a team to resolve problems, individuals will prefer to 'do it alone'. Instead of following a routine instruction from a supervisor or manager, the question will be asked, 'Why?' Individuals become suspicious when they are selected to do something over someone else, or vice versa, and this will start to reflect in their working style. Some people try to churn things out alone without running it by the manager, others run to the manager with everything. Some people decide to try to make an impression over the manager's head by making sure that their manager's manager knows everything that is happening in the department. Still others will sit back and start to work at a slower pace with an emphasis on extra detail in order to ensure that things are getting done in the best way possible, or because they are so distracted they cannot concentrate.

In short – the way people work after the announcement of a change programme will never be the same as the way they worked beforehand. Whilst that is not necessarily a bad thing in itself, it is certainly something that can represent a challenge for an Asperger leader, since often we may become confused by the way people have started to act differently, or not recognise that the people reporting to us now have different expectations for their own treatment which we may not be meeting. This issue will be addressed in a number of places as we proceed through the book.

Productivity suffers

Reading the above section, the observation that productivity suffers is pretty apparent. The lack of productivity, however, is not always malicious. It can be purely because people now have an increased workload as a result of the change process that takes them away from their business as usual. The focus of the individual and the focus of the team will, of necessity, move from the usual routine to what needs to be done to change. Deadlines and overall output may very well suffer as a result.

Unless a change programme has been very well orchestrated, most change exercises will result in a temporary loss of productivity of one sort or another.

The challenge, as a leader of change, is not to focus on eliminating loss of productivity, but rather to ensure that any lack of productivity is kept to as short a period of time as possible, and that there are contingency plans in place to deal with the side-effects. This is covered in Part 3 of the book.

Communication suffers

You will see one theme repeated throughout this book, and I re-emphasise it here – communicate, communicate, communicate. Potentially the most devastating side-effect of a change programme is a loss of communication. This can take the form of loss of communication between individuals and their manager or loss of communication within the team, all the way up to loss of communication between departments and across the organisation as a whole.

During a change programme, people don't want to hear platitudes about how things are going to be okay, this is the way to go, we are moving with the market, and so on. They want to know the truth, and they want to know the detail as it is going to affect them personally.

As we all know, the challenge is that very often managers within the organisation just do not have the information to hand that people want answers to, or they are unable to share it until the change programme is further down the line. The result is disillusionment and distrust amongst employees, and the fertile growth of the rumour mill, or internal grapevine as it is also known.

In cases where communication from the top down is poor, the rumour mill becomes the key source of communication within the company, with people taking rumours passed along this way as a given truth.

Even where the communication from the leadership team has been good, communication within the departments and teams themselves could well continue to suffer due to the insecurities caused by the change itself (as detailed in the previous sections). Internal communication and inter-departmental communication could suffer to the extent that the company grinds to a virtual stand-still – it truly can get as serious as that.

This topic is covered in Chapter 14, where some of the key communication activities are discussed.

Commitment to the organisation and its goals suffers

It is fair to say that when people feel that they are being betrayed in some way or another, their loyalties decline. A change programme is a challenge to the psychological contract the employee has intrinsically accepted and expects to have honoured by the employer. The fact that this unwritten contract is not being honoured represents – in the eyes of the employee – a betrayal of the intrinsic trust he or she has placed in the organisation. As a direct result, the commitment of the employee to the organisation and its goals declines. The focus turns from the goals of the company to the needs and requirements of the individual.

In addressing this side-effect, it is often helpful to develop tangible objectives for individuals that are linked both to the objectives of the company and the individual needs of the employee. This is not such an easy thing to accomplish successfully, especially for us as Asperger leaders, and this topic is discussed further in Chapter 16 under the heading of programme management.

Key people leave

One of the worst-case scenarios – especially for yourself as a leader – is where your key people have had enough of the insecurity and lack of communication and decide to leave the company (more colloquially known as jumping ship). Apart from the obvious problem of having lost key skills and intellectual capital, the effect on the people who remain in the company can be devastating. A valuable employee has left the company as a result of the change – does this mean he/she knew something they didn't? Is the change programme going to have some serious downside that they aren't aware of? Did the person who left know that the change was going to fail, or that people were going to lose their jobs?

You can see from the above how even one key person leaving can fuel the flames of the rumour mill. But even if you as leader are able to reassure staff as to the reason for the individual leaving, the people who stay and see the change through will still – in all likelihood – have to cover the additional workload of the person who has left, or have to help train a new or temporary replacement coming in. This aggravates stress and can lead to additional dissatisfaction and frustration.

Some of the most successful ways of ensuring that you retain your key talent are discussed throughout the chapters that follow.

The organisation's culture changes

One final point to make in this chapter is to recognise that a change programme will alter an organisation in many ways: it could change its leadership structure; it could change its processes and policies; it could change its organisational structure and operational model; it could change its environment. But whatever else changes, the culture of the organisation is going to change.

If we embrace the organisational model discussed earlier of the organisation as an organism, we can say that change is a key part of the organisational life-cycle, where the organisation moves through various stages of development through conception, growth, establishment, decline and demise. As the organisation moves through these various stages of the life-cycle, the changes it needs to undergo are far-reaching and intense, encompassing changes in structures, processes and strategies (Bridges 2000). Your change programme may sit on the cusp of one of these key stage transitions, or it may be a minor one within a developmental stage. In any event, the result of any of these changes is going to be a change in the *character* of the organisation – be it as a whole or as a division or even department. The organisation will not remain static. If it does, then the change exercise has not been embedded in the company, and it is likely that people will revert to the old way of doing things.

The establishment of the new culture within the organisation will be the topic of Chapter 23.

Now that we have examined some of the effects of change on ourselves, the organisation and the individuals working within it, let us consider in more detail some of the areas where we, as Asperger leaders, differ from neurotypicals in general. These are personal attributes that most people with Asperger syndrome who hold senior positions in business tend to possess or display, some of which offer us a significant opportunity, and some of which can seen as inhibiting unless we address them early. It is worthwhile highlighting these areas to make sure you are optimally utilising your talents.

Keep in mind as you read through the following chapters that these skills are not meant to be utilised one at a time, or in isolation. They work best together, as an overall skillset of the successful leader of change.

PART 2

Some Defining Characteristics of Asperger Leaders and Their Relevance for the Change Process

Chapter 7

Characteristic 1

The Centre of Knowledge

If you are an individual with Asperger syndrome who has been diagnosed as an adult, it is highly likely that you would have already undertaken your own research into Asperger syndrome – its symptomology, prevalence and hypothesised causes. It is likely that you are quite familiar with a lot of the factual information presented about this developmental disorder and the way our brains function differently to those of neurotypicals. You will, in all probability, have spent a significant amount of time and effort researching this in your own way. If you were diagnosed relatively recently, you may very well be in the process of gathering your own information right now.

Accumulating factual information

You may be wondering why I am opening the chapter with this seemingly random observation. I have given this as an example that I believe the majority of you reading this – if you are an individual with Asperger syndrome – can easily identify with. How do I know this? People who have studied Asperger syndrome have identified that one of our defining characteristics is that we tend to have very specific interests, and when we do, we dedicate a lot of time to gathering and integrating as much information in this area of interest – often to the detriment of other interests or areas of responsibility. We like to understand and have all the information about things that interest us. Knowing 'enough' just isn't acceptable. We have to gather all there is currently available – and potentially spark interest in new areas of research by asking those extra questions. Asperger syndrome is something we have discovered affects us directly, that is important in our lives and therefore is very likely to be a focus for you right now. Hence my confidence you have researched it.

Tony Attwood, an acknowledged specialist in the study of Asperger syndrome, notes that adults with Asperger syndrome can accumulate an 'encyclopaedic knowledge of facts' (2007, p.179) and comments that the person can often become an expert in the special interest. This is an observation I believe most of us can agree with.

Let us now apply this characteristic to the business environment. As a leader in your organisation, it is highly likely that part of your success within your organisation relates to the level of expertise you have within your area of specialisation. Let us think of some examples here. It is probably not a surprise to hear that a large number of leaders with Asperger syndrome work within finance, investment and insurance – although these are by no means the only fields. These are functional areas that are highly structured, with high levels of corporate compliance requirement, and within which there is often a plethora of information that can be utilised for the company. Asperger individuals who rise to leadership roles in these fields are often seen as industry specialists, and also frequently go beyond what is expected for their particular role or company, such as becoming an expert at international compliance, and so forth. The amount of information that these leaders have accumulated, catalogued and analysed intrinsically has given them an incredible insight into their workplace, and this is recognised. In addition, as people with Asperger syndrome, they will also – in all likelihood – have done a lot of research and gathered a lot of pertinent information about the business sector as a whole that they operate within, since the external marketplace can influence their 'internal database' of knowledge relevant to their organisation.

I am certain that as you read this, you will probably be nodding your head and recognising that you have been someone who has focused on knowing all there is to know in your functional area in the business. After all – it is just the way we tend to operate.

'But surely,' you may ask, 'that is the way any leader in business operates? What makes us any different to them?' Whilst we may feel that most people probably do the same thing in respect of gathering, analysing and storing knowledge about the functional area they work in as we do, the reality is that most neurotypicals have to work really hard to keep up to date with and retain all the relevant information required for their leadership role. Unlike for us, this does not come naturally to most neurotypicals and it is something that they have to work at. Some people employ staff to do that for them and present them with the summarised information. They do not retain the level of 'raw data' that we do in their heads – as they often say of us, their minds just do not work that way. Therefore, they may be just as much of an expert as ourselves in their field when it comes to overall information, but should they be required to 'dig deep' for any reason, or to come up with a new solution that builds on the foundation of the full range of previous knowledge, this is something they frequently have more of a challenge with. They will certainly do so, but they will initially need to step back and 'revisit' their knowledge base, whereas for the majority of us, the information is just there – we don't need to revisit, we just need to reanalyse.

Without a doubt, this characteristic is something within us that should – in the majority of circumstances – be considered a significant asset. By using our 'encyclopaedic knowledge' within our specialist area of work, we are able to make more insightful decisions and often keep our company ahead of the competition. We are frequently the first to identify when things like pending changes in legislation are going to have either a positive or negative effect on the company, and we are often the people that others in the organisation think of when information is required.

Encyclopaedic knowledge – the downside

Given all its advantages, how could this characteristic be in any way a negative one? Perhaps the best way to think about some of the negatives is to give you a hypothetical example.

Case study: The perfectionistic specialist

Roger is a director of risk management within a multinational organisation. He was diagnosed with Asperger syndrome in his late 30s and has spent some time getting to understand the diagnosis and reconcile how this has played a role in his life over the years.

As a child, Roger had an intense interest in aeroplanes – his parents had, in fact, described it as an obsession. He had collected every possible book on the subject he had been able to afford (or got his parents to purchase for him), had watched television programmes, had done research in the library (the internet not being around in his youth) and catalogued intricate details of various planes, developing detailed statistics covering flight times, average lifetimes for various planes, and crash investigation information. He was known as a little encyclopaedia when it came to the aviation industry.

But this knowledge had come at a cost. Roger spent the majority of his childhood in libraries, classrooms and in his room doing research. He did not interact with others very often, and when he did he was not taken seriously, since all he wanted to talk about was aeroplanes and some of the fascinating information he had discovered that day, week or month.

Roger had been fortunate in that his interest in aeroplanes had been overtaken by an interest in economics when he started doing it as a subject at high school. He had always enjoyed mathematics, but this was different. There was so much to take in, so much data to consume and analyse, so much to know...

The transition to economics acted in his favour and he started to 'obsess' over everything relating to the topic, ultimately leading to his getting three A grades for his A-levels and a first in economics at university. From there he moved into the insurance sector and his career had taken off from that point. Roger had earned the reputation of being the person to go to if people needed something done since he would either have the answer straightaway or, if he didn't have it, he would go and get that information in record time. After all, from his perspective, if he did not have the information, that meant he had a gap in his knowledge base, and that was just unacceptable.

Roger had a tendency at work to be a loner, since he often had his head buried in a book or his eyes trained on the computer. He struggled to leave his work, even to attend departmental meetings, and became annoyed if he was interrupted. He also worked late into the night to finish a piece of research or work he was busy with rather than leaving it to be completed in the morning.

Additionally, he appeared to be making himself unpopular in meetings, although he had no idea why. Whenever issues arose that he could contribute to, he always did, and since he knew more than anyone on the subjects concerned, he was very factual about what he knew and how that was the best information.

Roger found that he sometimes became confused in meetings when he tried to continue discussions on a topic of interest, only to be advised that the meeting had already 'moved on'. In a similar way, he sometimes was told off by his director for not responding to emails or completing standard management tasks, such as performance appraisals, budget accruals and cost coding. Roger found this frustrating, since he never appeared to have time to do these tasks. It was more important for him to ensure that he was up to date with current developments in his field – surely that was what he was paid for?

I am going to provide a list of some of the negatives associated with this talent for accumulating factual information. See if you can identify where this had occurred in Roger's experience detailed above.

Intense focus in a single area

It certainly is apparent from the above narrative that Roger displayed one of the challenges we all experience as a result of our interest, and that is an intense focus on gathering information and data on a specific area to the detriment of other activities. Like Roger, as adults with Asperger syndrome, we frequently have to make the transition from a childhood 'obsession' to a work-related one. It is by making that transition that we become the experts that we are. But, as happened with Roger, that intense focus can result in our becoming 'blinkered' as to what is happening around us. We, too, can become so focused that we do not notice when conversations change to another topic, and also run the risk that we are focusing so much on our core competency that we neglect others.

Struggling to leave tasks

If a task we are undertaking relates to an area of interest, we can become so engrossed in it that we do nothing else. Very few jobs involve doing just one thing – we need to be able to multitask in some form or another. We also need to recognise that sometimes we become so attached to a project within our area of interest that we fail to acknowledge when it is time to give it up, be this in the form of leaving work for the day, submitting the final version of a report, or even acknowledging that the activity is not productive and needs to be stopped. We should be aware of our tendency to want to 'carry on' and find ways to temper that with a sound helping of time management!

Inability to accept not knowing everything

A related challenge is that we tend to be perfectionists when it comes to our area of special interest. If there is something more to know, we have to know it. If there is another book to read on the topic, we have to get it. If there is more research to be undertaken, we need to do it. If you are employed as an academic or a researcher, this tendency will not represent a problem for you. However, for those of us in the corporate or commercial environment, this need to know everything can be a hindrance to productivity. We have to be able to acknowledge at an appropriate point that this information need not cover absolutely all possible scenarios or available data, but needs only to be sufficient for the company's requirements if we are going to meet our deadlines or other constraints.

Difficulty focusing on other tasks rather than those in an area of interest

We may be exceptional when it comes to completing work and tasks in the area where we have our focus. However, we frequently really struggle to achieve the same level (or anywhere near the same level!) of enthusiasm for tasks that sit outside our bubble of interest. Mundane, routine or even just obliquely focused tasks are avoided or left to the last possible moment, and then are done in the shortest time possible so that we can get back to what we do best. Sound familiar? Unfortunately, as I said before, there are very few places where a member of senior management does not have some sort of task or responsibility that falls outside that interest bubble. However seemingly insignificant, time-consuming or irrelevant they may appear to us, they are of value to the business and deserve as much of our attention as those elements we are interested in. That's a challenge to accept – I know – but there are ways of ensuring what you do for these tasks is at an acceptable level and undertaken in good time. After all, that is all that the company expects from you. It is not necessary to excel in all aspects of your job, so long as you are not failing.

Resistance to other people's inputs

This and the next point are actually related, and frequently go together. Often, if you have a lot of information about your area of expertise, it makes it difficult for other people to make adequate contributions. People may attend meetings with you and make suggestions or offer insights, but you may find yourself correcting them or adding more up-to-date data. People coming to you with suggestions on how to possibly improve something you have developed could be met by resistance. After all, you know your stuff – they are still learning. Are they suggesting you don't know enough? Sadly, for many of us, this is a reaction we do tend to have – mistaking suggestions and attempts to develop ideas from a junior member of the team as a signal that they feel they don't know enough, or seeing it as a challenge to our knowledge.

Confidence being perceived as arrogance

When we regularly respond to other people's input in the manner described above, those people will start to perceive your reactions as a display of arrogance on your side, even if that is not what is actually happening. In meetings, you may be trying to help your colleagues or staff by correcting them or adding information, but what will actually be happening is that most of those neurotypicals will be feeling that you are undermining them, or 'showing them up' with your wealth of knowledge as opposed to the little bit they have. There is nothing wrong with sharing your knowledge – in fact it would be extremely detrimental to the business and your working relationships in the business if you tried to keep everything to yourself. However, it is being aware of how often you do this, the context of where you do it, and how frequently you do it to any one particular person. As a guide, for example, I would generally recommend that within a single meeting, you should not correct people on more than two occasions. Do not interrupt people to do this. Do not correct someone if the correction is not going to make a significant difference to the outcome of the discussion. If it isn't, you can always let them know the up-to-date facts after the meeting. They will appreciate your discretion. If you do need to correct someone, be polite about the fact that you are correcting them and try to help them not appear ignorant. This can be done by starting with 'I'm sorry to have to add something, but I think you may find that the price has now increased to…' or 'You wouldn't have been made aware of this yet, but just to add that…' By ensuring that you do not embarrass others by sharing your knowledge, the risk of being perceived as arrogant will be reduced.

Chapter 8

Characteristic 2

Above-Average Intellectual Skills

A common misperception from a lot of people who are not that familiar with Asperger syndrome is that having this equates to being a savant. Whilst it is certainly true that there are a large number of people on the autistic spectrum that are in fact savants, this does not mean that a diagnosis of Asperger syndrome makes you a genius.

However, it has long been recognised that people with Asperger syndrome have advanced cognitive abilities. Attwood notes that some children with Asperger syndrome start school with academic abilities above their grade level, having taught themselves a lot of information from an early age, either through books or television (Attwood 2007). Baron-Cohen noted that teachers often find that children with Asperger's are talented in understanding the logical and physical world, and recognising and recalling a high level of detail within information (Baron-Cohen 2003). However, both authors acknowledge that challenges appear as the child progresses through school, indicated by problems with executive function. This is evidenced by challenges in functions such as organisation and planning, self-reflection, time management and prioritisation, understanding abstract ideas and applying new strategies. It is these shortcomings in our executive function – to whatever degree applies to us – that create challenges.

Now most of us have learnt to find ways to overcome our challenges relating to executive function during high school. We have generally taught ourselves strategies to cope with difficulties in organising homework on time, dealing with subjects that are abstract, and taking the time to reflect on our work and what we do or say in class. I would be fairly confident that the majority of us have internalised these coping strategies early in our high school experience, and have adapted the same coping strategies to our workplaces.

I found it interesting in Attwood's book that he feels the construct of intelligence is something that has a very high value for people with Asperger's and we tend to admire people who are intelligent (2007, pp.324–325). He indicates that it means more to us if someone implies we are not intelligent than it does to neurotypicals. I can only speak directly of my own experiences, but I am very aware of the fact that this has been a very sensitive topic for me personally. Any implication that I was not intelligent (or was stupid) was taken very personally (and still is, if I'm honest). I believe that it is due to this identification with the construct of intelligence that we tend to strive to increase our knowledge, overcome any areas where we have become aware of shortfalls, and continually test ourselves in respect of our knowledge-base. I am certain that most of you can identify with the reaction that I have if I hear about some relevant piece of information of knowledge without having been aware of it beforehand. My immediate reaction is annoyance at myself, then an intense desire to go out and internalise that information. Not knowing it would mean I am not doing what I should as far as my intellectual library is concerned.

To be fair, a lot of this is also linked to the fact that we tend to have very intense interests, as mentioned in the previous chapter, and that most of us do tend to experience a type of perfectionism with regard to performance. It is either good or bad, complete or incomplete, intelligent or stupid. Black or white. No greys.

Over the years, most of us have learnt how to develop a 'continuum' outlook in respect of the world (yes, there *are* 50 shades of grey…), but often we fail to apply this thinking to ourselves. We retain that element of 'perfectionism' in what we do. As a consequence, we do tend to exercise our intellectual muscles more than most. If we were to take the standard IQ tests, we may very well score quite highly.

The point I am making here is that as a result of the way we have had to develop our own unique coping strategies for acquiring, retaining and utilising information in a way that is appreciated by the neurotypical world, we have generally needed to flex our intellectual muscle more than others. This gives us an advantage when it comes to situations where we need to have access to our combined knowledge at short notice, or to be able to share information within a short time-span.

Additionally, because we have had to learn to apply these techniques as coping strategies for times when we have been under pressure, these strategies for learning and maintaining information are unlikely to desert us during a change programme. Most neurotypicals, on the other hand, struggle with 'brain-freeze' due to the pressures of change, and do not know how to cope. Whilst there is no doubt we also undergo pressure as a result of change, the experience of 'overload' is not new to us, and therefore we tend to jump to coping mechanisms almost automatically, and resolve the overload far quicker.

As you will see as you continue to read (you may already have noticed), this is a major advantage for you – provided that you are aware of the overload issues arising before they overwhelm you.

Chapter 9

Characteristic 3

Social Dichotomy – Social When
Necessary, Loner When Able

Let me start this chapter once again with a common misperception about people with Asperger syndrome. We are often seen as loners and anti-social geeks. We are the people who sit alone at the back of a classroom, or alone in a library at university rather than joining in any activities, or who sit in front of a computer all day, never interacting with others voluntarily.

Now far be it for me to counter that no one with Asperger syndrome fits this profile, for there certainly are some who do. However, I would also argue that there are a fair number of neurotypicals who would fit it as well. In fact, I know a few personally. However, I do believe that for the majority of us who have developed successful careers in the business place, this is no longer an appropriate reflection of our behaviour.

In order to be successful in business and to move up the corporate ladder into a leadership role, it is absolutely critical that you are able to work with people, be it in a team, as a subordinate or as a manager. At school and university this was less important, although for many people with Asperger syndrome, they have started to develop a 'social face' before leaving school.

It is certainly true that social relationships are more challenging for us. I used to find that understanding others – especially other females – was like trying to understand a plant. In fact, I felt I communicated far better with animals than I did with people. At least with animals I could interpret their 'moods'. If a cat purred at you and kneaded you with its paws, it was indicating contentment and security. It wasn't putting on a show of being content and secure whilst actually being angry or fearful. With people, you just never knew…

Having spoken with other leaders with Asperger syndrome, I find that a large number of us started working with the impression that our sociability was really not that important in the workplace – what mattered was our outputs. Unfortunately, in most cases this just isn't the case. Performance appraisals will reflect on an individual's performance both individually and as part of a team, and a whole section will be devoted to how well they work with colleagues and communicate with them (both vertically and horizontally) and to what others think of them. For anyone with Asperger's seeking to develop their careers, learning to become more social in the workplace is just a given requirement.

Many people who have worked with me and have subsequently been told I have Asperger syndrome are genuinely shocked. 'I would never have known!' is a phrase I have heard more than once. This is largely because I have taught myself to be social in the workplace – interacting with colleagues, training myself to notice things happening around me that I would not normally take notice of ('Jane is very quiet today when she is usually chatty – I need to ask if she is all right', 'Mark arrived in a new car today – I need to ask him about his new car', and so forth). I have taught myself to have a sense of humour (I concede to having learnt a lot from my daughter in that respect), to focus on making people feel good, and on encouraging people to believe in themselves. If I said that all came naturally, I would be lying. Whilst I may *want* always to have a sense of humour, always to know what to say at the right time, and make a difference in people's lives, I have not always intuitively known how. I have learnt by mimicking behaviours that I have seen work, by watching television shows that show people being humorous, and by studying psychology.

What I do at work every day is a conscious effort – over the years it has become more practised and easier to do – but it is still something I have to make the decision to do, every day. Once I am home, that 'face' disappears, and I can be myself. Now, in some cases, that can mean that a person could become a bit more of a loner in their own time, as they find the time to recover their energies after a busy day of 'socialising' at work. But for most of us, we have families with whom we enjoy spending time with. Yes, it is likely that we will need some quiet time before we become social again, but the level of being social in your personal life is unlikely to be as high as your daily work experience. Your personal social life is experienced on your terms, and there is generally less need for you to focus so hard on being 'neurotypical'.

So why am I mentioning this characteristic as one that is important to consider during a change programme? Well, the reality is that once a change programme is under way, your need to focus on your social and communication skills and strategies at work is definitely going to increase. It will become far more intense than it normally is. That is not to say that you will not handle it, because I believe with the correct approach to change (as I share with you in this book) it is something we can handle quite well. However, the reality is that if the amount of social interaction and social 'effort' increases significantly for us each day, we are automatically going to require more recovery time after work. So whereas before a change programme we perhaps needed the equivalent of the train-ride home alone as a recovery period, or half an hour before dinner, now we may find that we need more time to be alone. As a consequence, personal relationships can suffer if parties are not aware of what is happening and why. After all, if you are married with children and find that you are now coming home and cannot communicate adequately with your family during the week at all, but only really over the weekends, this is going to create tension.

If you are aware of how much time you normally take to 'recuperate' from your social 'face' at work, and you are aware of a change programme starting, you can be proactive and discuss the potential effects of the change programme with your partner. Together you can agree strategies to handle the situation. You could decide, for example, that in the short term you will not visit family members or friends as often as you usually would, or that you have a dedicated alone time when you get home before spending some time with the children. I have no doubt that your partner will support you during this time, especially knowing that you recognise how your behaviour may be affected and that you cared enough to discuss this with them before any problems arise.

Needing time to recover from the pressures of work is not unique to people with Asperger syndrome. Perhaps what is unique to us, though, is our need to isolate ourselves or go into overload if we cannot. It is important, therefore, that, rather than trying to get by on the same amount of recovery time you usually have, you build some spare time into your day to ensure you are able adequately to 'defuse'.

Chapter 10

Characteristic 4

Need for Personal Space

One of the symptoms frequently associated with Asperger syndrome is that of sensory hypersensitivity, as discussed in Chapter 4. Most of us have learned to adjust our environments to take into account our individual sensitivities, or have found ways to cope with our challenges. For example, I wear ear plugs if I am going into an area where there are a lot of people (such as the underground, a cinema or a canteen) and I wear specially tinted lenses at night so that I do not get blinded by the headlights of other cars.

As a result of these hypersensitivities, we tend to be individuals who need our personal space more than most neurotypicals. Often we find it difficult to work in open-plan offices or in teams, or in enclosed offices under fluorescent lights. We value our own areas being away from others to an extent, and often prefer being near windows or some form of natural lighting. Of course, in today's work environment, it is becoming relatively rare to be able to have your own office. However, there are often more formally closed-off areas for senior managers (such as the glass-wall office!). Whatever your work environment, you will have learnt how to adapt in order to work optimally.

During a period of change, you will need to be aware that it is likely that your hypersensitivities may be affected. Heightened levels of tension or pressure can result in senses becoming even more acutely sensitive than they normally are, and we need to be able to compensate for this in some way in order to ensure it does not result in any unnecessary overload issues for us.

This book is not going to go into the detail of how we can deal with hypersensitivities as such, since I believe this to be a specialist area that requires more space than I have available. However, we need to recognise that our sensitivities do exist; we need to understand what they are, how they affect us and how we manage them.

Think about your own sensitivities. How does your hearing, sight, smell or sense of touch relate to others you know of? Do you need to avoid loud conversations, avoid bright lights, struggle to read from white paper or monitor backgrounds, or tense up when people are near you?

Once you have been able to identify which hypersensitivities you have in your life, you need to think about how you have learnt to adapt to or cope with them over the years. This may sound obvious, but frequently this is not something we have consciously done. We have adapted our lifestyles to minimise any discomfort we may be experiencing, not necessarily as part of a formal strategy to address it, but by default. Something we did helped us, and as a consequence we have just carried on the way it is. Sometimes I have asked the question 'What did you do to cope with your hypersensitivity at work?' only to have the response 'I don't really know' or no formal response at all.

Part 4 of this book includes an exercise to help you think about your hypersensitivities and what coping strategies you find work best for you.

During a change programme, as I say, it is important for you to be aware that there is at least the possibility that these hypersensitivities will be aggravated. In order to be able to manage them, you first need to ensure you recognise the symptoms of your senses being overloaded. This is part of what I will be covering in Chapter 13. I recommend you have a look at the exercise 'Handling Your Reaction to Change' in Part 4 before reading Chapter 13.

Chapter 11

Characteristic 5

Delegation Challenges

Frequently, as a result of our intense focus, we become proficient at doing things ourselves without help or input from others. At school, we tend to prefer to work alone, because we know what we are doing and how we think. Working with other people at this stage creates challenges because some people in the group tend to be slower than others, or need things explained to them more often. For us, if we understand something, we just want to get on and do it, not talk it over all the time, or wait for others to catch up. As a result, we get frustrated. Sometimes we will have just gone ahead and done what needed to be done without waiting for the others. At other times we may have just lost interest in the work altogether due to the frustration we have experienced.

As we have moved into the workplace, we will have had to learn teamwork skills. Depending on the types of jobs you have held, the degree to which this was necessary will have varied. Some jobs allow you to work predominantly by yourself, with only an infrequent check-in with the team; others require you to work with a team on a daily basis. Once you move into a supervisory or management role, teamwork is a given.

Part of developing skills in working as a team is learning to share responsibility for work with others. In general, this skill does not come naturally to us. We prefer to be responsible for something from beginning to end. By doing so, we have complete control of what the outcome is, its quality and its content. When you share responsibility for pulling together an output (be it a presentation, a product or a discussion), you are relying on others being as enthusiastic about something as you, and having confidence that their contribution will be comparable to your own. I have already mentioned that one of our key characteristics tends to be that we are the centre of knowledge. Therefore, sharing responsibility with someone that we 'know' does not have as much information as us is difficult. Perhaps to some neurotypical readers that may sound like an arrogant comment. It certainly is not meant as one.

From our perspective, we are thinking of what is best for the company, and we are thinking about it logically. After all, if you went to a horse race with a number of your own horses, wouldn't you enter the fastest one to run rather than 'relaying' several who may actually be slower than the fastest racing horse you own? To us, this is illogical. In the neurotypical world, it is called teamwork.

Your career progresses and you learn to internalise all the requirements necessary to be a successful part of the team. Now you move into a managerial position of someone sort and have to learn a new skill – delegation. The stronger your ability has become to share responsibility in a team, the easier it will be for you to be able to delegate. Delegation is passing your responsibility for something on to someone who reports to you – together with the responsibility for its quality, timeliness and content. It also requires that you trust the person to undertake the task appropriately, and that you give them the space to do so.

For people with Asperger's, this is sometimes daunting. We don't like to let go of things that ultimately we have accountability for, and unless we are 'kept in the loop' we may feel threatened in the sense that we have lost control of something. As a result, we may actually start to undertake one of the worst management practices there is – micromanagement. Micromanagement is where we do not give our employees the space to be able to do their work. We check on them too much, ask for feedback too frequently, tell them how to do things, challenge what they are doing. Micromanagement can have a very negative effect on employees. It makes them tense, and they feel that you do not trust them. They will also grow resentful of your interference, no matter how good your intentions. I remind myself of how this may feel for them by likening it to the feeling I have when people come and lean over me at my desk. For me this is the worst kind of violation of my personal space – it makes me feel oppressed, threatened, tense and defensive – irrespective of the reason for the person being there. If you can identify with that feeling, you can probably empathise with how neurotypical individuals feel when they are micromanaged.

Another bad habit that can start to occur is that instead of delegating, you start to instruct. Rather than giving an employee the opportunity to own a task you have delegated, you effectively tell them when, where and how to do it. Let me give you an example. You call one of your direct reports in and explain to them that you need to communicate to the business that a roadshow is being held in three weeks' time that you would like to participate in. You ask her to come up with a plan and related budget, and give her a deadline to come and discuss her proposal with you by the end of the week. This is positive delegation. However, if you had called her in, told her about the roadshow and then told her to set up an intranet site, draw up some memoranda for staff and circulate them, get a videographer to come in and record an information session with you, etc., what you are doing is *instructing* them on what to do. It is very likely that the employee concerned will feel undermined and insulted by this, since you are not providing her with the opportunity to take on any responsibility, but are instead telling her step by step what to do. This implies that either you do not trust her or feel that she is incapable of thinking for herself.

A final area where a problem can start to appear is in the area of what I call 'dumping'. This is where you 'delegate' an area of responsibility to a subordinate, usually a more junior subordinate, but leave this with them as an ongoing responsibility with very little feedback or review. This sort of action can result in an employee feeling stressed, confused and taken advantage of. They can feel they are doing part of your job for you with no acknowledgement, support or feedback. On our side, what we have effectively done is handed over an area of work that is not one that we generally prefer to focus on, and then have effectively wiped it from our minds in order to concentrate on more important things. Whilst there is nothing wrong with handing over a responsibility, the difference between delegation and dumping is that in delegation there are agreed targets, reviews of performance and an identified outcome. It may well be that you agree to the person continuing with the work, but if you do, this will require regular feedback and review meetings in order for the employee to be able to ask questions and actually develop in their role.

Now, I recognise that as a person with Asperger's who holds a leadership role in your business, it is highly likely that you are already very comfortable with the process of delegation and have been doing it for some time. However, it is important to recognise that during a change programme and its related tensions, it is very probable that some of your standard coping mechanisms and ways of operating may need to be reviewed. Very often, due to the uncertainty of a change environment, a leader with Asperger syndrome may actually find themselves starting to micromanage. Worse still, they may progress to actually failing to delegate, or 'roping in' those things that they had previously delegated. The response is one that I prefer to think of as 'hugging to the chest'. When it is so important that things are done properly, we tend to revert to our thinking as people who are a bit perfectionistic, who know that we probably have more knowledge or skills than our more junior staff, and hence we should use those skills that are the best. We revert to our logic and abandon what we have internalised about teamwork and delegation.

During a change programme, you need to ensure that you are aware of your actions, and can identify if you are starting to show signs of 'hugging to the chest', 'instructing' or 'dumping'. In Part 4 of the book I have included some tools to assist you in this process.

Chapter 12

Characteristic 6

The Natural Leader in Times of Crisis

Yes, I do believe that people with Asperger syndrome can be natural leaders in times of crisis. I have seen it happen often enough. But let me clarify what I mean when I say this, and the reason for my proposal.

I want to start by recalling our typical reaction to an unexpected change as discussed in Chapter 4. Certainly, we will react negatively to unexpected change or crisis – as would any neurotypical. However, we do have the advantage over neurotypicals that once we have resolved the conflict internally, we are able to move on far more easily than most neurotypicals. Once the conflict is resolved for us cognitively, that is it. We do not need to go through another round of emotional resolution or analysis. It's done – we move on.

Another advantage that we have is that when we evaluate a situation, we are evaluating it logically, not emotionally. Again, let me clarify. I am not saying that the situation may not be affecting us emotionally. However, during an analysis of the situation in order to decide the way forward, we are able to view the situation through impartial eyes and determine appropriate next steps. Let us consider a crisis situation that we as people with Asperger syndrome can potentially identify with.

Driving home from work on a quiet road, you round a corner to be confronted with a traffic accident. Two cars have collided, obviously just before you arrived. Your initial reaction is that you are confronted with an unexpected change to your routine (you normally drive home this way, arriving home at around 6:30pm; this has interrupted your route and will delay your arrival at home). Most of us will experience some sort of reaction, be it frustration, a minor overload, a brief shutdown. However, we will have learnt methods to adapt to these, and they are likely to kick in within a very short time.

Once your coping mechanism has come into effect, you are likely to jump immediately into a practical mode. Your thinking may be along the lines of:

- The cars are in the road and there is a bend: I need to be aware of any other traffic coming.

- One person is already out of her car and very vocal, but the other person is still in his car: the second person may need some attention.

- There is the potential for injury: I need to call emergency services.

- The woman from the first car is in the road: she is at risk; she needs to get to the side of the road and sit down.

- One of the cars is still running: the engine needs to be switched off to avoid a fire.

At that time another car comes around the corner and stops. You get out of your car and call to the driver of that vehicle to warn any other cars coming to slow down, and ask his passenger to call emergency services. You also call over to the woman in the road that she is in a dangerous place. You tell her to go to the side of the road – you will come and speak with her in a moment. You then go to the car with the engine running and switch it off. At that time, you see that the driver of the second car is an old man and he appears to be disorientated. He wants to get out of the car. You immediately recall your health and safety training at work, and reassure the man that everything will be all right, but that he needs to stay in the car and remain as still as possible. Staying beside the man, you notice that the woman from the other car is walking around and shouting about how annoyed she is at the damage to her husband's car. You reassure the man once more, and remind him to stay still, then quickly walk to the woman and tell her that she needs to sit down and remain calm. You remind her that she has been in an accident and that she could have hurt herself, and therefore she needs to remain still. You suggest that she calls her husband calmly to let him know she is all right.

You return to the man in the car and sit with him until the emergency services arrive. When they do, you explain to them what you witnessed, what you did to secure the scene, and the injuries you noted on the man. The police thank you for taking control of the situation.

Now, I am aware that some people will say that it is a bit of a generalisation to say that most people with Asperger's will react well in this sort of situation, and the example I have used above is a bit dramatic, but the points I wanted to make were the following:

- We already have coping strategies for unexpected change that most of us are quite familiar with and can make operational within a fairly short time.

- Once we have our overload or shutdown reaction under control, we are able to analyse a situation logically rather than emotionally.

- Once we have logically determined the action to be taken, we are able to act on this – we don't tend to get tied up in emotional issues or politics.

Another point to make is that when there is a crisis situation, most people will look for a leader. If there is someone who starts to take control, most people will automatically take directions to help out. Take the man in the car arriving just after you. You instructed the man to warn any approaching traffic of the hazard ahead and for his passenger to call emergency services. It would be very unusual if the man had turned around and said, 'Don't tell me what to do! No, *you* watch the traffic and I will go and see to the man.' Rather, the people responded to the leadership you were displaying in taking control of a difficult situation. Certainly, the man may have been a doctor, and the situation would have been different, but in general your leadership would have been followed.

If you consider the work environment now, we once again have a situation where you could potentially be ahead of your peers or staff when it comes to being in a position to move forward after hearing about a change programme. Yes, you will also have the negative reactions. But, as already explained, you are likely to be able to move forward far more effectively once you have understood the reasons for the change, the possible effects of the change and where you are going. Once we have overcome our initial reaction, we are the ones who will start to examine the situation logically and rationally, not being directly affected by emotions and the psychological implications of the processes. Most neurotypicals will become very inward thinking during the initial part of a change programme, whereas we tend to just think of the programme itself.

An important point to make here is that whilst it is certainly an asset that you are able to think clearly and logically about a situation to determine the best route for you or the company to take, it is important that you acknowledge what other people are going through who are not so fortunate as to be able to distance themselves from their emotional interpretations of the situation. You need to acknowledge it, not necessarily change your plans because of it, but people need to understand that you know how it is affecting them. On occasion, you may find it necessary to alter a plan to take into account the emotional interpretations of employees. Unless you are aware of how people are reacting or will react in the future, you could make a change programme more challenging than it needs to be.

PART 3

Key Skills for Successfully Living and Leading Change

Chapter 13

Key Skill 1

Understanding Yourself and Your Reaction to Change

As mentioned earlier in the book, change is going to impact you as much as (and potentially even more than) some of the people you are aiming to lead through the process. It is essential that you both understand how the change will be affecting you (as discussed in Chapter 4) and how to put into place strategies to handle these effects and put them to good use, wherever possible.

Preparing for change

Many people I have spoken with have told me that they have spent a lot of time trying to prepare themselves for change by reading up on change management as a process, and learning how best to put together change management programmes for their staff. Whilst this is useful, it is certainly not necessary to fill your head with a library full of change management technique manuals in order to be successful.

Perhaps the first step in preparing yourself for change is to examine in more depth exactly what is going to be changing in your own work environment. A change is happening. Where is it taking you to? Why is it taking place? What will you be leaving behind? What should you make sure that you do leave behind, despite misgivings or challenges? What should you ensure you bring with you, despite it being easier to leave behind?

Let us look at these questions in a bit more detail.

Where is the change taking you?

Change programmes can take various shapes and sizes within organisations, and have a number of very different objectives as success criteria. Not only do you need to understand where the change programme intends the organisation to move to, you also need to understand where the change programme is going to take you as an individual. So, for the organisation, you need to understand such questions as:

- What is the change programme going to do to the size of the organisation?

- Are there likely to be increases or decreases in headcount?

- Is there going to be a fundamental change in corporate strategy?

- What is going to happen to the current corporate culture (e.g. is there another company involved in the change exercise)?

As a leader in the organisation, you will need to be able to answer the following types of question for yourself:

- Is this change programme going to result in your staying in the same department or moving out?

- Is it going to result in a change to your role at all?

- Is it going to require you to learn some new skills (e.g. in a new software system), or is it going to require that you give up some of the skills you currently have?

- What is going to happen to your direct reports?

- What is going to happen in respect of your own reporting line?

It is very important for you to have a clear vision of what the future is intended to look like, because it will be up to you to explain this vision to the people you are leading through the change process. A key step in preparing people for change – as is detailed in Chapter 15 – is to provide them with a vision for 'the way it will be'. You will need to decide on what is the 'positive vision' that you are going to share with your team, even if an organisation-wide vision has been communicated from the top down. The reason for this is that your team will look to you to interpret the messages coming down from the top, and to make these more specific to them. People want you to help them forge personal goals – and you can only do that if you have gone through the process of fully understanding where you need to get to, why and how.

Knowing that your team are going to be looking to you to be the 'interpreter of change', you – as the change leader – need to ensure that you have the necessary resources and assets to fulfil their expectations. Make sure you ask the questions beforehand that you know you will need answers to; make sure you call in those favours from key colleagues in the organisation; make sure you have the key contacts in place to ensure that you are kept in the loop in respect of the progress of the programme at senior management or Board level. In essence, get yourself ready.

Ask yourself the question, 'If I was being told of this change exercise five/seven/ten years ago when I was at the same level as my staff, what would I have expected my manager to tell me?' Your current subordinates would expect you to answer no less – in fact perhaps more – than you would have expected from your own manager. Make sure you can answer the questions.

Why is this change taking place?

Once again, if you are going to explain this to the people you work with, you need to understand it yourself. What is the objective of this change programme? Why was it initiated? Was it as a result of increased competition? Falling profits? Expansion? Downsizing? The answer to these questions can significantly affect the way the change programme is communicated and the way the change programme can affect both you and your team.

As I have stated before, you need to be completely clear where the company is going, and knowing what precipitated the change is essential to this. Ask yourself the question, 'What kicked off this change programme and – as a result – what is the specific goal we want to achieve?' If you cannot answer this confidently and completely, I suggest that you find some time with the senior management of the company in order to get the question clarified in your own head.

What should I take forward and what should I leave behind?

For me, the answer to this question lies in an examination of attitudes, and constitutes an important change in your role as a leader of people. If you are going to be successful in leading others through a change process, you will need to be the one who sets the example and lets people see that you have encompassed the change programme and its related ambiguities (Clarke 1994).

When a change process occurs, attitudes, ways of working, mind-sets – many of these have to be discarded and left behind. You need to work through the change and recognise – for yourself – what needs to be discarded and what needs to be kept. For example, you may need to discard the mind-set that success in the finance department means having an office, but you need to retain the attitude that higher than average performance is a key to success.

By examining your own attitudes, your own behaviours and your own mind-set in respect of the pending changes, you will have a much better understanding of the emotional and intellectual issues other people will be facing when the announcement is made to them (Buchanan and Boddy 1992), and you will be in a far better position to guide people through the change.

Knowing where you stand
What are the main opportunities and threats that may affect me directly?

Understand that if you are going to lead a change exercise successfully, you need to make sure you are completely honest with yourself about what both the opportunities are for your success and the risks are for your failure as a change leader. It will not do your team any good to be half-way through an extensive change project only to have their leader and mentor drop out.

The opportunities for you in the change process are usually much easier for you to examine and internalise. It is delving into the threats that can be a challenge. So how best can we do this, and what sort of things should we be looking for?

The greatest types of risk in respect of change are those of your own behaviour and attitudes. This is because they are often the most difficult to recognise and subsequently change. What are your attitudes on change? What are your underlying assumptions about business and how the organisation should operate? Asking yourself these types of question will give you a great deal of insight into how you personally will react to changes you will be required to make.

Essential to getting the most out of this exercise is to be honest with yourself. If you can, ask people close to you what they see in you and your personality. Be open to the good and the bad. If you can identify personality traits that could be a hindrance to you in the change process – whilst it is unlikely that you would be able to change them in the time before the change starts – at least you will be aware of them and how they affect you. Recall the issues discussed in Chapter 4 concerning how people with Asperger syndrome can react to stress. Try to identify any reactions that you may have under stress and how you deal with them. Never underestimate the power of pure recognition in understanding behaviour.

Do I have the necessary technical skills?

As mentioned earlier, change programmes do tend to challenge your technical skills in certain areas, such as project management, finance and general planning.

It is a reality that no change exercise is the same as another, and therefore it is impossible to say definitively which skills are required and which are not. However, two areas which will certainly be invaluable for you are those of project management and finance. Without a doubt, if you are implementing some sort of a change programme, you will be making use of some sort of project planning during the programme. You may not be the person doing the project plan, or even a key member of the project team, but it is true to say that in this field it is very worthwhile understanding the mechanisms behind the process so that some of the technical talk doesn't get in the way. The same can be said for finance. Financial management plays a part in every aspect of business, either directly or indirectly. Even if you feel that the input in this area may be minimal for this particular project, there will certainly be other situations where the skills will come in handy, so any training will never be a waste.

With this in mind, it is strongly recommended that – if you have the opportunity – you enrol yourself on a one-day project management course, or buy one of the short 'how-to' series of books on project management. Generally, project management training courses recognise that managers undertaking the course are about to initiate some sort of change programme, and as a result they do tend to cover some elements of change in the training. This can be a useful extra.

Is my professional network up to date?

If you don't have time to invest in formal training, now would be a good time to look at your professional network and see if you have contacts with the skills you require. Very often, they will be more than happy to spend an afternoon with you running through the basics.

Apart from the abovementioned benefit, updating your network within the organisation at this time is also very important. This can help you with such things as communication and professional support – very often in change programmes one person will get to hear things before another. If relationships are renewed, this information will be communicated if your associate realises that it will affect you. If you do not update your professional relationships or network, it is possible that the same people may not realise that the information they have received relates to you.

Leaders going through a change process succeed most frequently when they have access to an inner circle in their network. This is a small circle of people within the organisation that you can work with closely and with whom you have complete confidence. These are the people you can confide in, get advice from, rely on to support you in your change efforts, and for whom you would be happy to do the same. These people may be people from your own department, or may be from across the organisation. The point is that they are the individuals you will bounce ideas off and rely on for input and intelligence in respect of the change.

If you already have an established inner circle, make sure that you informally review their strengths and attributes in respect of the situation you now find yourself in. For example, someone who has been a member of your inner circle for a long time could actually be someone who is very set in their ways, or dedicated to the current organisational culture of the company. This person will be of little help to you in the change programme, and could end up holding you back or creating more stress than they help relieve. Don't be soft in this area – if the person has the potential to derail your change programme, they really cannot be considered part of your inner circle any more. They would, instead, be a colleague or associate – the relationship has changed.

How strong are my people skills?

This brings us to an area where challenges may exist for you as an Asperger leader and which – if you haven't already done so – you need to prepare yourself in order to be successful. This is in the actual role of the people-manager in the change process.

Managers used to have their roles defined as purely directing and controlling staff, resources and information. However, this has been changing over the years to encompass the role of facilitator and coach. A manager is now better recognised as a person who leads, facilitates and motivates people to identify the need for, as well as achieve, change in the business (Mabey and Mayon-White 1993).

Now more than ever your people skills are going to be tested, and it is acknowledged that Asperger leaders often do not have strong people skills. In preparing yourself for change, therefore, make sure you spend some time examining your own competence in this area. If time permits, invest in a training course or a short mentorship programme of your own.

The following chapters focus on key skills that are largely people-related, since I believe that this is the one element of the change process where Asperger leaders could do with some additional development.

Chapter 14

Key Skill 2

Making Communication a Focus

Communication is one of the most critical elements of a change programme in an organisation. It truly can make the difference between the success and failure of that programme, or whether the change continues post-implementation. In actual fact, communication is an important part of preparing your people for change, but also needs to be happening throughout the change process, not just at the beginning and at the end. It is an ongoing and critical success factor. This is a very broad topic, and what I will be covering in this chapter is, as far as I am concerned, the minimum amount of information that you require in order to make your change successful. However, I would recommend that you perhaps invest some time in reading additional books on this topic if you are able.

As leaders with Asperger syndrome, we have learned to adapt to the requirements of business-as-usual communication within the workplace. Without a doubt, it is an area you will have had to work at and develop your own strategies for. It is interesting that a number of leaders with Asperger syndrome I have liaised with have indicated that they had to learn to overcome challenges with issues of communication *before* they had been diagnosed as having Asperger syndrome (and I include myself in this category). We realised something wasn't working as well or intuitively for us as it appeared to be working for 'everyone else' and therefore took steps to address this. For some of us, this involved observation and mimicking of successful communicators, for others it involved formal training programmes, and for others it involved buying libraries of books on the topic and developing their own strategies; for some it involved a mixture of all or some of the above. You were invited to think about such decisions in the previous chapter, and it is important to keep these developmental strategies in mind as you consider helping others cope with change.

So why is communication so important in the change process? The answer to this lies in the fact that a period of change is a time when people are feeling insecure and are desperately seeking clarity and reassurance. People need now, more than ever, to have their questions answered and their concerns addressed. Having open and active communication with those people involved in a change process is fundamental to their coping with the risk and ambiguity this process will be introducing into their lives (Pugh 1993).

There are several components to the communication process, and we will cover a number of them here. However, the extent and exact nature of your communication efforts will largely be determined by the type of change initiative you are undertaking. For example, the type of communication required for the announcement of a company merger is very different from that required for the introduction of a new computer system, and the span of communication required for the announcement of a re-engineering programme is very different from that of a departmental restructure.

Beckhard and Harris (1987) developed a useful hypothetical formula to represent key elements for implementation of a successful programme. According to this formula, change (C) happens when the product of the levels of dissatisfaction with the status quo in the company (D), the desirability of the new vision or proposed change (V) and the effectiveness of the first practice steps of the change progress (FS) are greater than the resistance to change itself (R). Representing this as a mathematical formula gives us:

$$C = [D \times V \times FS] > R$$

Beckhard and Pritchard (1992) added to this model, introducing the construct of Believability as being another element to add to the bracketed element of the formula, and De Woot (1996) additionally added Capability (Figure 14.1).

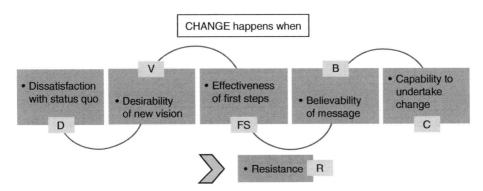

Figure 14.1 Elements of a successful implementation of change

This model reflects, for me, just how important the communication process is. An understanding of the new vision, the believability of the proposed change and the success of the first steps of the change programme are all intricately intertwined with the communication process.

However, looking at a change programme in general, there are a number of communication elements applicable to all situations, and which need to be considered in more detail. These are:

- the first announcement

- the ongoing communication during the programme

- the wind-down communications.

The first announcement

The first stage of preparing your people for change is actually communicating that change to them. We are working from the premise here that you will be the first person to communicate the impending change to them, and the discussion that follows is based on that assumption.

The way that a major change is communicated can make or break that initiative. Many leaders communicating a change programme are extremely skilled in pulling together all the information needing to be shared with the employees of the company in respect of facts, vision and method. Bridges (1991) suggests that most managers are very well informed when it comes to the mechanics of change itself, but are often unaware of the dynamics of the psychological change cycle as discussed previously (or what Bridges refers to as transition). Where many leaders feel challenged is in dealing with the emotional and psychological elements of the announcement. I would say that, as Asperger leaders, our challenge is not so much handling the emotional and psychological elements of the announcement, but *recognising* these and correctly *interpreting* these reactions in our people as well as in ourselves. In addition, we need to ensure that we are adequately 'displaying' our own appropriate emotions – energy, enthusiasm, passion, excitement, sincerity.

It isn't sufficient to stand at the front of a company gathering and read from a prepared document, factually detailing what needs to change and why and exactly how you intend to do it. In fact, doing so would do nothing more for you as leader than brand you as cold-hearted, unemotional or detached from the 'troops'.

Yes, there are key messages that you need to get across. But just as important as the factual content of the message is the way that message is communicated and your implicit acknowledgement of the effect of the announcement on your people. Even if it is only to the extent of saying, 'I understand.'

People need leaders they can identify with and look up to. In order for people to identify with us as leaders with Asperger syndrome, we do need to make the extra effort to make sure that the way we appear during a change programme suits neurotypical expectations.

Let us now look at what needs to be communicated and how that needs to be done.

The content of the communication

There are four key messages that do need to be factually conveyed in your initial communication session. These are:

- What is the situation?

- What are the effects of this situation?

- What are we going to do about it (and how – the change programme itself)?

- What is the ultimate goal of the programme?

It is important that you fully understand what the situation is in order that you can clearly and unambiguously explain it to your people, as well as being able to answer any questions addressed to you. This will help to avoid any misunderstandings or frustration down the line.

People need to understand the effects of this situation and what is creating the need to make a change. Very often, leaders advise employees of the circumstances at the root of the change programme, assuming that people will logically understand the link between this and the reason for the change. Don't make that assumption. Even if your people do make the link, they will be reassured to know that their interpretation is the correct one. So, for example, explain to people that the reason you are introducing the new procurement system is that it will ensure that the company controls its costs better, or that the reason for introducing a new vehicle tracking system is to ensure that clients are kept informed of delays and therefore will not take their frustrations out on the driver. Once again, the more you can clarify a situation to avoid confusion or misinterpretation, the better.

Clarifying what you intend to do to address the situation that needs to change is important in giving a visible purpose for introducing an uncomfortable change environment.

The manner of the communication

In communicating the facts about the change initiative, it is important to keep in mind that you are communicating with people who have just had their psychological contract challenged in one way or another. To put it another way – they will become wary and suspicious almost immediately. They will be in the midst of those very complex and intense emotions that accompany change – no matter how well the impending change is communicated, or how potentially positive the final state is meant to be.

In speaking to clients in respect of communicating the first message, my advice is to keep the following points in mind:

- Put yourself in their place.

- Address people personally.

- Address all levels of employee involved, not just management.

- Be open and transparent.

- Don't be afraid to share your feelings.

- Try to keep the message straightforward and short.

- Be aware of potential cultural differences in the way the message should be communicated.

We have already discussed putting yourself in their place, but it is worthwhile reminding yourself of the feelings involved in receiving this sort of announcement shortly before you give it. This will increase your empathy with people who react negatively, and thereby help you not to counter-react.

As far as addressing people personally, what I mean here is that announcements should be done in person. Do not rely on sending out corporate emails, webcasts, notices on the intranet or making an announcement in the company magazine. These things should be used as secondary information that is sent to employees as a follow-up, not as the first communication itself. Many people need to be able to ask the questions that spring to mind as an uncomfortable announcement is made. Others find reassurance in being able to look into the eyes of the person making the announcement. Making an announcement in writing is invariably seen as cold and sometimes cowardly – the person did not have the 'guts' to face the music. It can also give the impression that the company does not care about the employees enough to schedule time to speak to them directly, or that they have something to hide.

It is acknowledged that very often it is just not viable for you to be able to address all your people directly – you could be the Chief Executive of a global company with over 250 branches. In this situation, make sure that you pull together members of your global leadership team to undertake the direct communication in the various regions, but still try to ensure that you undertake as many personal ones as you can, for example one in each continent, or by means of a webcast.

Recognising the importance of personal contact can make the difference as far as the programme is concerned. I once consulted to a medium-sized organisation that was introducing a very significant change initiative that would have a very direct impact on all the people across the organisation. When I advised the Chief Executive that it would be best for him to make the announcement directly to his staff, he shook his head and stated that there was no way he would be able to do that. Intrigued, I asked him to clarify why he felt that way, since I was aware that the company only had approximately 1000 people across two sites.

'Well you see,' he explained, 'it is all down to the nature of our business. Due to our operations, we have to have people available 24 hours a day, Monday to Friday. We achieve this by having four shifts. You can't expect me to present to people across four different shifts…'

As it happened, we did eventually arrange for the Chief Executive to present to his people across four shifts over a four-day period, and their positive response was noted by the initially sceptical CEO.

In the same way, do make sure that you take the time to address people at all levels in the organisation. If you are a chief executive or company president making an announcement about a pending merger, very often it is tempting to make the announcement in person to your leadership team and senior management teams, and then leave them to do the rest of the communication. Sometimes this is necessary to a certain extent – especially in global companies, as mentioned above.

However, there is always a way to ensure that the message gets communicated by yourself down through the organisation personally. Examples can be that a number of personal presentations are scheduled at various times and sites, with video-conferencing available to all staff. One of my clients organised their announcements to be done as a live teleconference and webcast that all employees could watch and then ask questions through a dedicated call-in centre or online forum. Some organisations do not see that level of communication as being necessary, and feel employees would be quite happy to watch a recorded version of the announcement on the intranet or on a DVD. You know your organisational culture and need to make sure your approach is appropriate.

Perhaps the one point that leaders tend to hesitate on concerns transparency. Frequently, senior leadership in the company are of the opinion that it is not appropriate to communicate all the details of the change programme in the beginning, feeling that this will confuse employees or result in people jumping ship. Often it is considered a confidentiality risk. The reality is that the better people are informed, the less risk there is for the strengthening of that corporate monster – the rumour mill. Be honest with people if you do not have all the answers at that time. People will appreciate your being honest and saying, 'I don't know the answer to that question, and probably won't for at least the next few months.'

It is a very challenging invitation to managers to share your feelings, but this can be a very powerful tool. There is nothing wrong with being open with your people about how you personally feel about the changes to come. Share the fact that you are excited about the new system to be introduced, or that you are reluctant to move from a comfort zone. So long as the right message is communicated as part of that sharing, being open will help others to identify with you as being in the same boat, and not see you as an authority figure imposing change on them whilst remaining impervious to the change themselves. Note, of course, that I am not encouraging you here to be over-emotional or dramatic. That will certainly not inspire the confidence of your team! Being aware of how much you want to share and how this could influence people is something that you should think about beforehand and be comfortable with before the announcements are made.

Perhaps a very obvious consideration is that the message itself should be short and to the point. We have all heard the acronym KISS (Keep It Short and Simple). That certainly applies here. People what to know what is going to affect them directly, and they do want to understand the detail. But once an announcement is made, people do not want to stand (or sit) around for hours whilst the strategy of the company is discussed. Instead, they want the chance to ask the questions and then go away to take all the information in.

This brings me to the final point. When you are thinking about communicating the message – especially where you are communicating it across a number of sites or countries – do make sure that you take into account the culture to which you are presenting. A message that goes down extremely well in one presentation could cause an uproar in another, purely due to the use of words which have a different connotation in another country or community. Be aware of your audience. If you are not sure, get advice either internally or from an external adviser. The best way to make sure that you are saying what you intend to say is to ask someone from the target population what they think of your message.

A final recommendation for you at this point concerns the period of time just after you have finished making the initial announcement. It is standard practice to allow a 'Question and Answer' session at the end of the presentation. In the case of announcing a change programme, this is even more critical. It is important that you encourage people to ask the questions that they have, rather than leaving them bottled up inside, even if you know that the questions may well be uncomfortable or difficult to answer.

I generally recommend that the session is ended with the invitation for questions. Once the questions from the room have ended, invite people once more. If there are still no questions, encourage people to go away and think about the announcement made. Empathise with them in respect of their initial feelings and acknowledge that they may need to go away and discuss this with their colleagues and families, but then provide them with the avenue to address the questions at a later stage. For example, have a follow-up meeting in a week's time, or have a queries email address, or a questions page on the intranet. So long as there is some mechanism by which the questions that you have invited people to raise can actually be answered. Keep in mind, as well, that the best way to answer these questions remains personally, so it may be that a follow-up meeting is scheduled at a defined date in the future, or that a meeting be scheduled when a certain number of questions are received, and so forth. Provided people know and are comfortable with it, the exact mechanism for ongoing questions can be what suits your company best.

The ongoing communication during the programme

I have seen a number of organisations put in place some absolutely brilliant initial communication programmes for their change projects – far above what was needed to be effective – only to have their overall programme fail dismally due to no actual plan for ongoing communication.

I am not going to go into a detailed breakdown of what the ongoing communication should look like. The point I am making here is that there does need to be ongoing communication in respect of the programme at a group/company/departmental level. Given your leadership level within the organisation, the following generic recommendations should be adapted accordingly.

Make sure communications are regular

It is very important to ensure the communication in respect of the programme continues regularly, even if there is no significant information with which to update staff. The fact that you are potentially being open with staff to say that no progress has been made since the last update will generally be received far better than silence. It is consistent with your message of transparency and openness – whether the news reflects positively or negatively on you.

You will also find that the fact that you are undertaking to communicate regularly will certainly provide intrinsic motivation to try to ensure that unnecessary delays do not occur. After all, how many people want to explain why they haven't achieved what they said they would?

Having said that, it is also important to avoid making the communication a monotonous, repetitive event that people would much rather avoid than hear. I strongly advise that you speak with your corporate communication team (if you have one) to get some ideas about keeping the communication relevant and 'alive'.

Ensure bottom-up communications, not only top-down

Poor upward communication has been identified during management research as one of the six silent killers that block change and learning in an organisation (Beer 2001).

At the beginning of a change programme, it is standard practice for the company or department leadership to communicate the information concerning the change programme down through the organisation in a general announcement, and that is how it should be. However, subsequent to that, many leaders start to communicate ongoing information down through their direct reports (generally senior management), who act as filters to the information before it is cascaded further down. This is referred to as *top-down communication*. In the majority of cases, this works well, in that irrelevant or sensitive information is 'removed' before being passed to less senior employees. In a case of change communication, on the other hand, this filtering of information is not what you want occurring if you are going to be following a programme of open and transparent communication. Managers who take it upon themselves either to 'shield' their teams from what they perceive to be difficult information, or to communicate only information that suits them, are acting as gatekeepers within the organisation. The only way to have open communication within your organisation going through change is to minimise gatekeepers by ensuring communication is made to all levels of staff on a regular basis (Hayes 2007).

Another issue with continuing to communicate in this manner is that information takes a long time to travel from the top of the organisation to the bottom – if it even reaches the bottom at all.

Morrison and Milliken (2000) speak about the problem of 'organisational silence'. This is a paradox where most employees know the truth regarding certain issues and problems but are afraid to voice to superiors, for a number of reasons. As a result, upward communication is blocked by the same gatekeepers that interfere with downward communication.

Therefore, it is important at this stage that the company initiates a programme of *bottom-up communication* as well as the ongoing downward communication. This is undertaken by presentations being made to the junior staff of the company, generally through the employee unions, forums or councils. This information then filters upwards at the same time as the information presented to management starts to filter down, thereby ensuring that all levels of the organisation receive the information at the same time or shortly thereafter. It also ensures more consistency in the information being communicated, thereby reducing the possibility of miscommunication due to over-filtering.

Horizontal communication

Just as important as the upward and downward communication discussed in the previous point, we need to ensure that there is communication across the organisation. Different departments and divisions need to communicate with each other, and it is crucially important to ensure that you avoid departments/ divisions entering into a sort of competition to ensure that their area performs better than another. Hargie and Tourish (2000) emphasise that unless there is proper horizontal communication with departments and groups working together, there will inevitably be feelings of isolation, dissatisfaction and low levels of involvement from staff.

If you are divisional or departmental leader, ensure that you make an effort to ensure that you initiate some horizontal lines of communication with other areas – suggest cross-functional team meetings, regular change programme meetings, informal cross-functional communication.

If you are on the leadership team of the company, be alert for signs that any of your departments/functions is becoming isolated. Encourage the development of cross-functional teams by asking for change-related feedback from a cross-functional team.

Ensure it is a two-way process

The final point made here has been touched on previously, but I would like to emphasise it. When you communicate information to your people on pending changes, do ensure that you make the communication a two-way process. This applies not only to the initial communication, but throughout the programme.

You need to ensure that there are mechanisms in place for people to be able to communicate back to you, be this directly or indirectly. This can be the ongoing Q&A sites on the intranet, or regular update sessions where people can ask questions personally, or an automated telephone line where comments from people can be recorded and forwarded either for information or for response.

Communication is a special activity we undertake both on a formal, company or department-wide basis, as well as on an individual basis with people in our team. Checking throughout the programme that this is something that we are taking into consideration will help us to make the change programme flow better, and will assist us in preparing our team for the change to come.

The wind-down communications after implementation of a change programme

What is very important to understand is that the post-implementation communication does not purely consist of an announcement that the change is complete. Post-implementation communication needs to be ongoing for a while after the change programme, sharing the results of the change, the new environment and culture, the successes and what the company has learnt. It needs to be an ongoing celebration of the success of the change.

There is nothing worse for employees than going through the stress and additional effort of ensuring that a change programme is successfully implemented, only for their efforts effectively to 'dissolve' from memory within a few weeks of the change programme having been successfully completed. I generally advise leadership teams to ensure that they have a post-implementation wind-down communication plan covering a period of at least six months. Some organisations work this ongoing communication into their regular internal communications.

We will discuss some additional considerations in respect of the transition cycle in Chapter 24 and communication issues relative to this.

Chapter 15

Key Skill 3

Preparing Them for Change

In starting the discussion of preparing your people for a change programme, it has to be said that by far the most essential part of that process is communication. I know I have emphasised this point quite a lot so far, and I will reiterate it again and again as I continue, but I honestly cannot overemphasise how important proper communication is – not only as an overall corporate exercise, but at divisional, departmental, team and individual levels.

The Asperger's advantage

I would like to spend a few minutes here thinking about the differences between ourselves and neurotypicals when it comes to some of the key parts of change. We have already covered in detail some of the areas where we, as Asperger leaders, may experience challenges with change. Often, we make the mistake of thinking that we have the monopoly on experiencing stress during change. The reality is that we don't, especially not later in the process.

As I emphasised in Chapter 4, once we are able to understand and internalise change, we frequently manage it very well. We have accepted it, we have adjusted our thinking to orient towards it, and we are in coping mode. When it comes to neurotypical individuals who are faced with a change programme, although they tend to be better configured to handle this initial information better than us (they do not appear to get as stressed, they do not generally suffer 'shut-downs' or 'explosions', and they do not experience sensory overload issues), neurotypicals do tend to cling to the past as much as (and sometimes even more than) we do. For many people going through a change programme at work, this is the first time they have had the experience of not being in a comfortable place, of not exactly fitting in, of having to find coping mechanisms to get through. In these areas they are amateurs compared to us. These are the kinds of challenges we have faced our entire lives – the fact that we are where we are today shows that we are the pros!

When I started undertaking change and transformation consulting, I was confused by the way people in the workplace just seemed to fall apart in change programmes (speaking very generally, of course) and how they needed to be reassured over and over and over again. Messages needed to be repeated, clarified, repeated, emphasised, repeated, and then repeated again. Over and over. Personally, I found this behaviour to be rather strange. I had learnt by this time to cope with change – after all, it was part of what I did for my work and it was how I had grown up. Once the change situation was explained, clarified and the direction made clear, I was able to focus on that, internalise it and make it my new reality. Once it was clear and understandable – it was clear and understandable! I did not need the message repeated over and over again. After all, it had been explained to me, I understood it, I accepted it and I kicked into coping mode. What more was there?

I realised at one point that it might be a good exercise for me to think about how I used to handle change before I became more adept at teaching myself coping strategies. As a child and young teenager, it was far more challenging for me to handle change. It felt like a violation of my space, my existence, me. I would not accept that the change could be beneficial, despite any detailed explanation that may have been given. Let me use an example.

At one of the schools I attended, one of the formats for learning was that of a type of open-learning, modular system. A student was able to select a module of work for a subject area (in this case mathematics), complete it independently on the computer and with workbooks, and on successfully passing the module test, move on to the next module. The student was able to choose the order of the modules, how many he or she completed, and the level of work. I loved this way of learning. It suited my learning style, being visual and individual, and I soon had completed all the modules up to what was then O-level standard, although I was only in my first year of high school. My maths teacher was very impressed, and I discovered – to my horror – that the learning programme had only been intended as a trial and would be ending that year. Needless to say, that did not suit me, since I had adapted to learning this way and enjoyed it. My teacher told me that due to my performance, I was being admitted to a fifth-form maths class so that I could start to prepare for taking O-level Maths. My teacher explained that this was a great opportunity for me both to get an early qualification and continue to progress with my studies in a subject I enjoyed. The alternative was to join the rest of my form in a general first-year maths course. He asked me if I wanted to go ahead. At the time that he explained this to me, I was overcome by the change this represented, but I did understand the positives. So I agreed.

The next week, however, when it came time for maths, I made my way to the computer science room where the modular studies had taken place, and sat at a monitor. The programmes had been removed from the computers by that time (they did not have the capacity in those days to keep redundant systems on machines), so I just sat and stared at the machine. Over and over, my maths teacher would come and find me, clarify where I was supposed to be and why, and take me to my new maths class. Time and again I went to the computer science room. Of course, I understood that this no longer was an option for me to study maths, but that was irrelevant to me. It represented what I knew and enjoyed, and I did not want to lose it.

Ultimately, my maths teacher told me that if I did not stop 'messing around' he was going to report me to the headmaster and have me 'demoted' back down to the normal first-year maths class. This didn't deter me, but fortunately I did not end up being referred to the headmaster since my parents decided to move again, and I ended up in a new county in a new school, learning maths I had already taught myself over four years ago. It wasn't a happy time – but I had to learn to adapt.

As the above example shows, as a young teenager I refused to go with a change, despite the fact that I understood its ultimate value for me. I had to have the message repeated to me over and over. Each time, at the point that the message was reiterated, it made sense and I went along with it. But within a short time of the discussion being over, I was already resistant to the change again. The point is that I needed to have the message communicated to me over and over to help reassure me and try to help me realise that my 'rebellion' against the change was not going to stop the change taking place. But I continued to rebel against the change because it disrupted the comfort-zone I had established, and forced me to leave something I had enjoyed in the past.

I have realised that, for a lot of neurotypicals, going through change programmes is a very similar experience. They are frequently frightened by the change and are often desperate to remain in a place where they feel comfortable and secure. Whilst they may understand and agree with the change programme when it is first explained to them, they quickly revert to that resistant outlook once the communication wears off. If the reasons are communicated again, they will be positive about the change for another short time, before again reverting to a 'rebellious' or resistant stance – trying to hold on to the way things were.

In short, they do not have the necessary coping mechanisms in place, and they have no comprehension of how to develop any. This is where we have an advantage, and can help them cope.

Helping them discard the status quo

One of the most fundamental actions in ensuring that a change programme is successful is to move your people from their current place of comfort to where you need them to be. But to do that we need to get people to recognise the need for change and to discard the status quo. This step may have been covered by your first general communication made to the group, or this could be something that you want to cover with your team directly. Whichever way it is done, you need to ensure it actually happens, since any new behaviour can only be successfully adopted once the old behaviour has been discarded.

There are a couple of ways of doing this. Rubin (1967) recommends that this is done as a confrontation: set the information in front of people in such a stark and indisputable way that there can be no doubt that a change is necessary. Kotter (1996), on the other hand, recommends creating a sense of urgency – getting people to understand that there is a pending situation which needs addressing and which needs addressing *now*. Personally, I think that Rubin's method tends to be more successful for those of us with Asperger syndrome. We need the logical facts, the black and white, the understanding of the reason for change, how we will do and where we are aiming to get to at the end. This helps us orient towards our new behaviour and vision, and we focus our coping strategies to direct us there. For us, Kotter's approach of creating a sense of urgency can, I believe, be counterproductive. It can create anxiety as we realise that this has to be done – NOW! – and that there are related tensions, deadlines and threats. It is the *or else* part of Kotter's approach that I believe to be negative for us, since it makes us tense and defensive, and we can often close up or shut down.

Neurotypicals, on the other hand, I believe react better to Kotter's approach than Rubin's. If you put stark reality in front of neurotypicals, they tend to get defensive and angry, perceiving this as a threat rather than an opportunity to change. They enter panic mode ('Oh my gosh – our sales last year declined – I'm going to lose my job!') and start to focus on escape and protecting their bubble. On the other hand, presenting a change scenario as a chance to address an issue that needs to be addressed now will often make neurotypicals sit up and acknowledge the need for the change ('Gosh – to keep our market position we need to improve sales this year. We'd better get this new sales programme in place').

Whichever approach is ultimately taken, however, the objective is to 'unfreeze' people – get them to start moving from the position they have been frozen in for so long. The following are some of the key ways to ensure this takes place.

Direct team communication

Whilst the group announcement is an important one, there are things that can be done within your own team or department which are very important to this process. You need to spend the time making people see why it is necessary for them to change and to start the process of committing to that change. As you have seen in the psychological change cycle, it is highly unlikely that an individual will hear the news that change is necessary and immediately be ready and eager to make that move. It is your responsibility to ensure that you are giving people the time and communication space to be able to move from numbness and denial to at least the phase of contemplation.

Openness and transparency

In spending the time communicating to the team, you need to ensure that you are open and transparent with them. Questions will often be asked over and over – not only because people need to be certain that things really are the way you say they are, but also to test you. It is human nature for people to be suspicious when bad news or changes are announced, no matter how positive a relationship you have. As leaders with Asperger's, this is something we may find hard to accept, and see it as a reflection on our relationships with people. You need to be reassured that this is not a reflection on you or your communication skills. If you have adequately prepared yourself for the change communications and have followed the advice presented here, you can be confident that what is happening happens to most change leaders – it is not a result of any shortcoming on your side. Neurotypicals (and yes, even some people with Asperger's!) will need to be reassured over and over about the reasons for the change, that it is the right thing to do, that it is actually happening, that it can't be reversed, and so forth. Take it as a normal result of a change programme.

Being open and transparent all the time is hard work, there is no doubt about it. But it is worth the effort in the end, especially if you think about the side-effects of not doing it. If we are not transparent about the change, people will continue to be suspicious throughout the change programme, and will automatically consider any delays or problems experienced in the programme as an inherent fault in management's thinking.

Acknowledge your shortcomings

There is also a second side to being open and transparent with your team, and that is being able to admit where you do not have all the answers. People in the organisation tend to see their leaders as having all the information and answers there could possibly be. When all the information they expect to be available is not communicated, people have a tendency to think that leadership is filtering or withholding information. On the other hand, if you are open with your team and share with them your own lack of knowledge or information, you will create a situation where your team will be better able to identify with you, or recognise that you can, in fact, possibly identify with them.

It also serves another important purpose, and this is in respect of leading by example. If you are dealing positively with a lack of information or knowledge, this provides a positive example to your people of how to deal with *their own* lack of knowledge and insecurities.

As part of this, you also need to be prepared to admit where you as a leader, or your leadership team, have possibly made mistakes or errors – either now or in the past. Individuals do respect honesty, especially when a leader is putting him- or herself out on a limb to acknowledge his or her own gaps in knowledge or skills.

Emphasise continuities

Another important skill for you as a leader of change is to provide as much stability for your team as you can during the change process. Some people may see this as a slight contradiction of an earlier recommendation, namely to encourage people to discard the old ways. However, this isn't a contradiction at all, since providing a certain level of ongoing stability will actually facilitate the ability to discard redundant behaviours.

If you consider once again the psychological change cycle in Chapter 3, you will remember that people go through a phase of insecurity when they begin to realise that the change is actually going to take place. This is related to loss of security and what is familiar, and the introduction of a sense of the unknown future.

At this time more than any other, people need certain continuities that can act as anchors for them during the ongoing change. What do I mean by continuities? I am referring to those parts of the current situation which will be retained, and against which we can reassure staff that not everything is changing. Examples may be in the form of certain processes being retained in the business (e.g. a new flexible benefits system is being introduced but the performance appraisal system is to remain unchanged), key people remaining in the business (e.g. everyone in your department is remaining in the department, despite roles changing), or the overall nature of the business remaining the same (e.g. the organisation is still aiming to be the employer of choice in the pharmaceutical sector).

By communicating to people that changes are going to be taking place, but that certain current responsibilities, processes, people or environments will remain unchanged, you are providing them with a level of reassurance that not everything has dropped out from beneath their feet. This will give them something to focus on during the ongoing part of the change programme, allowing them to let go of those parts of the current situation which are no longer required, yet retaining those parts that are the basis of stability.

Above all, it is important for you to be able to take the step towards putting yourself in their shoes. I know this is often something that can be challenging for us as Asperger leaders to do, but perhaps imagining a similar scenario you were faced with when you were young and still learning coping mechanisms may help you reconnect with those negative feelings change can create. If you were able to connect with your childhood or teenage self going through that change without coping mechanisms, what would you advise him? How would you reassure him? How would you encourage him? It is highly likely that some of that advice, reassurance and encouragement would be very applicable to your neurotypical staff going through their first change programme. Whilst I am not telling you to apply it directly to them (unless you feel this is appropriate), it is something that you should remind yourself of when dealing with the challenges of leading your people through change.

Chapter 16

Key Skill 4

Programme Management and Its Application

If the change programme is going to be successful, it is important that people understand what they are aiming for and what they have to do to get there. People need to have a vision of the future, something that they can identify with – at some level – and that they can ultimately make their own.

But it is more than purely creating a vision. As a leader of change you need to transmit to your people a sense of urgency in respect of the programme and a clear understanding of what has to change (Kotter 1996). As mentioned in Chapter 5, it is human nature to want to retain stability and security. As a result, when changes are announced in an organisation, people will always try to find a way to return to the status quo. This could be done either actively or passively, but whatever form the action takes, people are acting as an impediment to change.

Very often, the best change initiatives fail or falter not due to a lack of planning or setting of objectives in respect of the programme, but due to a failure to communicate that adequately to everyone involved in the change to the required level of detail. The leaders of the change teams have a wonderful vision as to how the change is going to improve the company, its competitive advantage in the marketplace, or its profit margin. Yet how to get from A to B has never really been thought about in detail, or if it has, the requirement for business as usual to continue has been overlooked in considering resources and time.

Project management: Complementing our Asperger skillset

Reading about people with Asperger syndrome in the workplace, we are frequently advised of our challenges, how to deal with our deficits and ways to fit in. In this book I am also aiming to assist people with any challenges they may be facing in the area of change within the workplace, but I also believe it is important to emphasise that we, as Asperger leaders, have a unique skillset that often gives us an advantage over neurotypical leaders. I have already spoken earlier about our ability to be practical and display logical empathy in situations of crisis and change (Chapter 12). Now I would like to emphasise another skill that we tend to have, and that is around noticing and being able to identify vast levels of detail.

When I first started working as a consultant, one of the areas I received direction on was that of how to draw up an effective project plan. I recall my supervisor's advice at the time that it was essential to start from the big picture and then work down to the detail. This concept confused me. Why would we start with trying to picture something we haven't even defined yet in terms of its component parts?

'Why would you do it that way?' I had asked.

'Because that way you ensure that you always have the final picture as the focus of your planning, and you can use that to work backwards to get to the steps involved in getting there.'

Far from explaining the situation, this confused me even more.

'But why would you want to do that?'

I recall that this question annoyed my then supervisor.

'Because there's no way you can start pulling together that amount of project planning without working backwards. You would get lost in the detail!'

I had learnt by this stage in my career when to continue to question and when to keep quiet, so I left this comment without response. I realised at that stage that most neurotypicals do need to work backwards when setting up a project plan, because they really cannot see the necessary amount of detail without working backwards in 'chunks'. Unlike most neurotypicals, however, most people with Asperger syndrome actually work most effectively when we work from the detail up. Unlike the average neurotypical who says, effectively, 'Okay, show me the big picture and then we can see how to break it up into smaller pieces, which we can then work backwards from', we tend to say, 'Okay, let me understand where you want to be, then let us start at the beginning, incorporating the details as we develop a path to that final state.'

I am not saying that we ignore the big picture. What I am saying is that we have learnt to develop a full picture through our cumulative knowledge about an area and what it consists of. Understanding where you want to be naturally incorporates an understanding of the milestones necessary to get there – at least for us. Let me clarify what I mean by this with an example.

If a group of people from your organisation were advised that the company was going to introduce a new calendar and email system, most of them would focus on the final product and what is different about it, before deciding what are the key steps involved in pulling together a programme of change. If we are presented with the same information, on the other hand, we tend to think more along the following lines:

- Our current calendar and email system is used in this way – x, y, z; the effects of a disruption to those uses can be restricted by…

- The running of the current calendar and email system is controlled by the IT team; a change in system would require a significant time commitment from their side; they are currently busy with another project; they need to ensure that they have the resources necessary…

- The current calendar and email system is used by the following departments…; the departments that are most dependent on the system being up are…

- The current calendar and email system has the following interfaces with the external customers…; the maximum down-time needs to be…; the most optimal time to do a change-over is…

In other words, we automatically start with the detail and start to build up our own mental image of the programme. I am not saying that we will have all of the information necessary immediately, but we will have the necessary framework to start populating our visual Gantt chart or project plan. For some of us, the entire programme plan can be visualised right from the start.

For most of us at this stage in our careers, this type of thinking has become second-nature and as a result we are often able to present quite detailed project plans quite early in the process, covering areas of the project that others may have not thought about. This is certainly an asset for a change programme. However, what we do need to ensure is that we have paid sufficient attention to the human elements of the change programme, as detailed in this book. That may require your making a special effort to identify 'human' issues in your visual project plan.

Do not underestimate the importance of showing that you understand the big picture and know where you are aiming to be. However, use your talent for discerning detail to pull together the project plan outline ahead of your programme kick-off. Remember to share that this is the high-level project plan, and that details will be agreed together with everyone concerned. The fact that you are able to share a relatively comprehensive idea of exactly how you can achieve the change will provide reassurance to your team that you understand some of the intricacies involved in the change.

From the above observations, it should be apparent that the first step towards leading a successful change initiative is to detail the process involved in the journey, who is involved and what their critical milestones are, and then to ensure that these are communicated to everyone in a way that is logical, understandable and actionable.

Setting the critical milestones

Planning for a change initiative is a process where there needs to be a balance between pre-programme planning and development of plans during the programme itself (Figure 16.1).

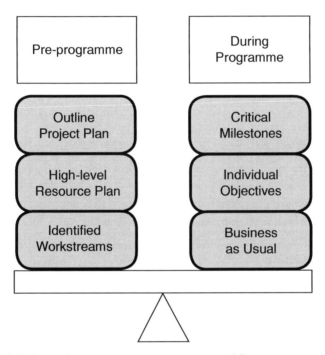

Figure 16.1 Balance between pre-programme and live programme planning

It should be understood that whilst it is important that sufficient planning is done before a change programme kicks off, this should not be done to such a level of detail that the change programme never actually starts. Although we want to ensure that we plan for as much as we can before initiation, micro-planning can be as disruptive to a change programme as micromanagement is to delegation. Planning before the start of the programme should be to an appropriate level of detail, but specific objectives for the teams and individuals need to be established as the change programme starts, so that the actual people playing a role in the change programme can be involved in the process. This book is not aimed at programme management itself, but if you have a programme management role as part of the change programme, I would recommend that you review some literature on this subject, such as *Managing Successful Programmes* published by the TSO.

It is important for your team to understand that ultimately the effectiveness of the change programme lies in their hands. They play a key part in the success or failure of the change, and as such they need to ensure that they take ownership of what they need to do to make the change happen.

As part of the planning stage of the programme, you should have developed a high-level project plan for the change, as discussed above, together with the key milestones. In starting the programme, these should now be shared with your team and the key activities relating to these key milestones developed.

Setting detailed objectives as a team

A number of managers feel that the change programme should be detailed up front and that people in their teams should just be advised of what needs to be done rather than going through this with them. In some cases this may be appropriate. However, I do believe that in order for individuals to buy in to a change programme, it is important that they are involved in the programme development in some way. Understandably, if you are a company chief executive, you are not going to be able to sit with all your employees to develop objectives, but you can have a kick-off meeting with your direct reports, as heads of functions, and take control of the downward communication of the change programme to their teams.

In some cases, especially in the case of multinational organisations, it is just not feasible for such detailed project planning to take place across all regions. Again, communication is critical here – a leader may not be able to have a meeting with all affected parties at one time, but meetings held can be recorded and communicated to any involved parties so that they are aware of what decisions are being taken.

Where a change leader is able to have a project kick-off meeting with his or her people, it is still important that the leader has taken the time to develop an outline set of objectives as a basis for development. There is no way that the meeting to finalise individual objectives for members of the change team can start from a blank page. You, as change leader, need to hold an interactive session with your team whereby you outline the project plan and objectives, and encourage feedback and revision where appropriate, rather than start from scratch.

Why do I encourage you to do it this way rather than purely assigning tasks and objectives? Once again, I emphasise that people are going through change, and as a result they are going to be resistant – to some degree or another – towards changes being forced upon them. If people are involved in the development of the key tasks and objectives, they are more likely to take proper ownership of those objectives and be more motivated to see the programme succeed.

Considering 'business as usual'

Make sure in developing individual and team objectives for the change programme that business as usual for their area is taken into consideration. So often we make the mistake of just assuming that we will be able to cope with business as usual whilst change is introduced. This is an assumption that should never be made, since change can often take up far more of your people's time than is realised. In reviewing workloads, therefore, take into account current responsibilities, as well as the potential for bringing in temporary support staff, if necessary.

The topic of temporary staff is, itself, an important one. Often, when it is acknowledged that additional support may be needed during the period of change, people in your team will strongly recommend that temporary people are brought in to do the work related to the change so that they can continue with what they know best. 'After all,' they often argue, 'it will take me so long to train someone to do this current job, the change programme would be over by the time he or she was fully up to speed.'

Please be aware that this is not a valid argument. Wherever possible, if temporary support is to be brought in, it should be to cover business as usual, and not the change elements. The main reason for this is that we want our people to be engaged in the change process. If they are focusing on business as usual whilst leaving changes with temporary staff, the changes to processes and thinking generated as the programme proceeds will be internalised by the temporary support person rather than your permanent staff member. As soon as the temporary support leaves, you will find things – by default – drifting back to the old ways of doing things, since your team members will have no attachment to the new way of operating and therefore no commitment to see it succeed.

Yes, it is true that time has to be worked into the plan to train temporary support people in the workings of the current system. However, it needs to be kept in mind that this is going to be a relatively short-term assignment and therefore the individual does not have to have an in-depth knowledge of the system, but rather needs to be trained in the areas which are simplest to delegate and which will free up your team member's time. For example, a temporary support person needs to understand how to operate a specific data-capture system. They do not need to understand why it is designed the way it is, or why we run certain reports.

Building your change team
Selecting the team participants

First and foremost we need to put the team together. In a change situation we are looking to pull together a change programme team largely from current employees rather than new recruits. They are likely to be from different departments and, depending on your level of seniority in the company, potentially some of them may not have a reporting line to you within the business-as-usual scenario. If there is a company-wide change programme taking place, it is quite possible that additional people will be recruited into the company who have special skills. If it is a departmental change programme on a smaller scale, you could have someone seconded to your department on a temporary basis to assist with specialist areas, such as project management, IT or human resources.

When you have responsibility for selecting new team members for a change initiative, there are a few things that are important to take into consideration when selecting the right people.

- The person needs to be confident and able to step comfortably into the new role. It does not help the change situation to bring in people who will need time and effort to settle into their roles, since the other members of your team will already be stretched with the additional work associated with change.

- Ideally, the person should be an internal change agent already, in that they will be able to inspire confidence in the other team members due to the fact they have been involved in this sort of experience before, and hence are able to encourage them through mentorship. I will discuss the development of change agents in Chapter 21.

- It is important to bring someone in who has the right attitude. You will have spent time preparing your team for change and ensuring that they have a positive outlook on the project. If the person you bring in does not reflect this same positive attitude or optimism, it could result in confusion and antagonism within the current team, and that is something you need to avoid.

Frank LaFasto and Carl Larson (2001) undertook assessments of over 15,000 team members in respect of their team-mates. Their observation following this research was that teamwork basically consists of four factors: openness, supportiveness, action orientation and personal style. If these are the factors that are important to members of the team, then it is important to ensure that they are considered in adding new members to the team.

Allocating roles within the team

Within standard team-building, a team leader has the time to determine who best suits which roles, taking into account things like personality, skills, experience, personal preferences, and so forth, before going out and sourcing those people. In an internal change programme, you are starting from a situation where the potential team members already work for the company, but temporary changes need to be made to their role. For example, it may be necessary to have some additional project work done within the department, and this will require you to allocate the role of project manager – for instance – to one of the members of your department, which he or she will need to do alongside business as usual.

If you are going to retain the commitment and enthusiasm that you have (we hope!) established within your team, you will need to ensure that the allocation of new roles and accountabilities within the team are agreed together. People tend to lose interest in jobs that they have just had allocated to them without discussion. If they feel that they are part of the decision as to who does what, this is far more likely to be acceptable.

What does need to be kept in mind, however, is that ultimately this has to be your decision. In some cases there are jobs that just have to be allocated, whether people indicate their interest in undertaking them or not. The key here is to encourage the concept of teamwork, which means that people work together to help each other to get what needs to be done, done.

Setting team goals

With a general team environment, the setting of team goals generally rolls smoothly from the allocating of roles within the team. Within a change situation this is less straightforward. If we are going to encourage people to stop thinking and acting introspectively, as they tend to do at stage one of the transitional cycle, we need to ensure that they are focused on the team and the teamwork activities required of their role. This can help people to see that they are not alone in being affected by the change programme, that they have a role to play, and that they are not isolated.

Once the specific objectives have been established for both individuals and teams, it is time to have a look at establishing the transitional rules of work for your people during the change programme.

Chapter 17

Key Skill 5

Establishing the Rules for Change

Whilst it is important to recognise that a change programme is going to be challenging for your people, it is also essential that they are given a very concrete understanding of the fact that the change is happening, no matter how uncomfortable that may be.

I think this is an important point to emphasise. Once again, it links back to communication, and the fact that this needs to be regular and consistent. As people with Asperger's, we may have internalised the fact and process of the change, but that does not mean that other people have. Largely due to our lack of 'mind-sight', we tend to feel that if things make sense to us and we are able to cope, that means that it should be understandable by everyone and they should be able to cope as well. I will refer to this point later on in the book, but for now it is important to remember that just because we understand the 'rules' for a change programme, where we should be heading, how we should be doing this and why – that does not mean others do.

Now, for many people, making the statement that a change programme is going to go ahead irrespective of individual employees' feelings may sound a bit harsh. But in reality, if a change programme is initiated by the senior management of the company, it means the programme has been debated as part of the strategy of the company and a formal strategic decision has been made. As such, this is not something that is going to be stopped, unless the senior management team decide to reverse their decision.

You may be part of the organisation's senior leadership team, in which case the above would be very apparent to you, or you may be the manager of a function within a department. Whatever level you operate at, it is important to understand and communicate the fact that this change is happening, and that the best option for everyone is to come along for the ride.

Nadler (1993) talks about the importance of maintaining control during a change programme, and discussed a number of what he calls 'transitional devices' for doing so. These include:

- developing and communicating a sense of direction

- appointing a transition manager

- developing a transition plan

- allocation of specific transition resources

- development of feedback mechanisms to facilitate monitoring and control

- rewarding transitional behaviours.

Some of these transitional devices were discussed in Chapter 16, but the point about the development of feedback mechanisms to facilitate monitoring and control is really what we are discussing here. The best way to achieve this is to initially establish some rules for the change.

The essential rules for change

The rules that are being put into place now are established after the communication of the change programme has been done and initial objectives set. This is important – rules can only be internalised once people understand what changes are coming and what role they are expected to play in making the change happen.

One of the comments I had from a client recently was that referring to the following elements as *rules* as opposed to *guidelines* was being too dictatorial. But the reality is that you *are* establishing rules as opposed to guidelines. To say that these are guidelines for the way people are expected to act during a change programme is far too vague, and allows people the opportunity to decide whether or not they feel they want to follow them. As we have said elsewhere in this book, ambiguity in change is negative and results in people becoming frustrated, holding back on decisions, and potentially lowering performance either consciously or subconsciously. The rules we are going to establish are intended to do three key things:

- Provide a sense of order in the midst of change – these are rules which will not be moving.

- Ensure that people become aware of potentially negative behaviours and how these need to be overcome.

- Provide a mechanism for the identification and potential elimination of disruptive behaviour.

If rules are to be established and accepted by the employees in the company, it is important that the employees buy into them. In much the same way as was necessary in setting the goals and objectives for the change programme, you – as leader of change – need to ensure that the team you are leading, either directly or indirectly, take ownership of the rules that are going to govern their behaviour.

The main difference in establishing team buy-in with regard to the rules is that they should already have bought into the goals and objectives for the change, and so should already be focused on the change goals. Unlike the development of objectives, however, many of the rules to be established here are – of necessity – going to be dictated by yourself. The key, then, to getting the commitment of the team to the rules for change is in transparency.

Once the objective-setting sessions have been completed, you should call your team together (either as a unit or – if you have a larger team – in a series of meetings) and outline to them the need to establish some rules for change. This is an important first step, since people do want to understand why they are being expected to abide by new rules and why these are being formalised rather than being informal.

The rules for change need to be explained as being the new ways of working that are going to be critical to the successful completion of the change programme. Emphasise how important this is, and how – consequently – these new ways of working cannot be seen as anything other than rules of work, not guidelines. In applying these, make sure that you can justify to your team why the introduction of control is important.

At this stage, you may very well have some people who are resistant to the idea. It is human nature to avoid restrictions or over-regulation. As soon as you mention the word 'rule' in a change situation, people become defensive. It is up to you as leader of the team to reassure them that although these are fixed parameters for the way things need to work going forward, they are being introduced as part of the process in order to help the team cope in a new situation. In the process of drawing up the goals and objectives of the individuals in the team, you should have gained a deeper insight into the psyche of the people working for you. This will help you in being open and transparent with them about the need for certain key rules.

We have spoken about how to tell people about the rules. So what exactly are these rules? Each business, division and department is different, and after reading some of the following example rules, you will – in all likelihood – be able to identify a number of additional rules which will apply specifically to your own situation. It is strongly recommended that you introduce no more than five rules for change in total, or your team will find themselves overwhelmed by controls and end up resisting the rules and associated changes.

Rules that could be introduced include the following:

- Documentation usually signed off by one person needs to be signed off by two during the change of process.

- People are required to use a time-logging system on the network whilst the new IT system is being reviewed.

- Any purchases within the company need to go through a new procurement procedure until the change process is completed.

- Budgets are frozen for the duration of the project.

- Hours of work may need to be more flexible during the project.

- Customer calls may have to be logged onto a special computer system during the process to ensure customer service standards.

- Any changes need to be communicated to the employees through the Employee Committee or Works Council.

I am certain reading the above examples has made you think of many more that are relevant to your own situation. These may be less formal, or perhaps more so. In any event, no matter what the interim rules are for your people, make sure that you explain to them the reason for the rule, the duration of time for which the rule will need to be in place, and thank them for their commitment.

You may also find that it is helpful to share with your team any rules you have established for yourself, or had established for you. In this way, people will be able to identify more with you as being part of the change team – your schedule has also been disrupted, not just theirs.

Another thing you need to ensure you do is to monitor the rules – make sure that people are following them, and if they are not, intervene. It is not fair to other people in the team if there is one person ignoring the rules whilst they are making the necessary sacrifices to make the change work.

Providing feedback

It is always assumed that as leaders we are familiar with how to provide feedback, and it is reasonable to assume that most of us will be. However, how do we deal with providing feedback to people who are not abiding by the newly established rules of change or the change programme itself? Here are some general guidelines for providing feedback to an employee of potentially negative behaviours or observations that they are finding things difficult.

1. *Before speaking to the individual, try to get some validation of your observations from other people in your team.* Remember that you will need to do this informally but also in a discreet way. Speak to members of your team individually and ask them if they feel there is anyone in your team who could do with some additional support, or who appears to be finding the change programme particularly difficult. If it is someone you are confident can be trusted with confidential matters, you could ask them directly how they feel the person concerned is holding up. Always ensure that the people you are speaking to understand you are asking because you are concerned, not because you are annoyed or frustrated with the person concerned.

2. *Make sure that you provide the feedback soon after the problems become apparent.* It is important that your feedback is not delayed, but addresses the situation in a timely manner. That way the feedback will be more effective since the incident will be fresh in the person's mind.

3. *Be objective in describing behaviour.* Generally, this is not an area that we have a problem with, but it is important to ensure that we use neutral words and do not describe behaviours in ways that will lead the employee to feel defensive or resentful purely as a result of how we phrased things. It is also important to ensure that the behaviours you are discussing are things that the person can actively change, either through improved performance or a change in attitude.

4. *Make sure that you have the details of the incidents to hand.* It is very important to be able to specify examples of what you are talking about, rather than saying things like, 'I have noted that your performance just seems to be below par.' Be specific.

5. *Mention the effects of their performance on you and on other people in the organisation if appropriate.* Let them know how you feel about the issue and the way it is affecting others.

6. *Make sure that the person clearly understands what the feedback covers.* There should be no misunderstanding of where the issues lie.

7. *Offer them the opportunity to respond.* Give them the chance to explain their situation, their interpretation or any other circumstances.

8. *Agree together how the person's performance can improve.* You need to be very clear about this. Ideally, you should document this informally (e.g. by

summarising the information in an email). Allow the individual an opportunity to be involved in deciding how to improve the performance.

9. *Agree a further review period.* Once the discussion is completed, agree a follow-up date and what behaviour changes you will be expecting to see at that time. The individual needs to be clear as to how you will be monitoring them.

Finally, I would say that your acknowledgement of their commitment in this situation will go a long way in maintaining the morale of the team. Never forget to recognise your people and what they are putting into the change effort.

Chapter 18

Key Skill 6

Motivating the Team – Challenges, Opportunities and Rewards

The details of the effects of change on people so far should be more than enough evidence to show that change programmes are hard on individuals. Even if you want to be positive in your outlook, it would certainly have to be said that change programmes are, at the very least, demanding.

We have already indicated how important it is to have realistic and tangible targets in place for people, and in this chapter we will examine the importance of recognising successes whilst acknowledging shortfalls against those targets. But people who lead the most successful change projects recognise the need to introduce a range of transitional devices to reward behaviour, including short-term wins.

So what actually are we talking about when we discuss short-term wins?

Defining short-term wins

The immediate definition that comes to mind is that a short-term win is something that acts as a positive reinforcement for people after a relatively short period of time. Whilst this is a good definition as far as it goes, let me ask you this. Who or what determines what constitutes a positive reinforcement? Are all forms of positive reinforcement of the same value to everyone?

Perhaps the best way to cover this is through a case study.

Case study: Flex system at Motlicore

Motlicore United (not a real name) was a large chain of DIY centres with stores nationwide. In 1999 it was decided that they would introduce a flexible benefits system for their staff, as well as a proper job evaluation system (since benefit entitlements were linked to grade). Meetings with the relevant members of the Human Resources, Finance and Operations teams, together with the external consultants appointed to implement the flex system, resulted in a project plan for implementation of the scheme. The challenge for the leadership team was that the plan had a two-year timeline, with results only being beneficial to staff after 18 months. However, in the interim period, there was going to be a lot of change taking place in respect of operating processes, policies, procedures and overall cultural change.

James, the Group HR Manager at the time, realised that unless staff had a reason to feel that this huge project was worthwhile, they could very easily take the easy option and jump ship to the new chain of DIY stores opening nearby and looking for experienced staff.

As a result, together with the external reward consultant, James came up with a proposal that enabled staff to be involved in and – more importantly – benefit from the programme throughout the implementation phase.

The way that they did this was to develop a highly interactive communication plan for the flexible benefits element of the project. This allowed an ongoing 'design forum' where anyone was able to go along and make suggestions about the potential flex design. Strict timelines were shared and enforced in respect of this to ensure that the project did not get hung up on communication.

As new benefits were agreed at the forum, these were introduced on an interim basis outside the flex system. For example, one of the items that was suggested as being valuable to staff at the company was a 'Collect and Deliver' laundry service at the office. This was investigated and an arrangement negotiated with a supplier to start offering this at the offices on a 'pay-on-the-day' basis until implementation of flex, at which point it would be converted to a monthly subscription from the payroll. This provided a very positive response from the staff, who were then far more enthused to continue with the change necessary for the introduction of the flex scheme (Bergemann 2007).

The above case study is a very obvious example of the development of short-term wins for the people in the company during a very people-centric project. What is appropriate, however, in change initiatives that are not so people-centric?

Take a merger project. This type of change programme – whilst generally being exciting or motivating to the leadership of the company – tends to do very little for employees further down the line. In fact, these can be quite devastating experiences, depending on how they are handled. How can we find short-term wins in *this* type of situation?

The answers to the above questions can best be determined by first asking yourself a series of questions.

1. *How long is your change programme?* The length of your change programme can make a big difference in deciding on the frequency of your short-term wins. If the change programme is due to last between three and six months, your short-term wins should really start to appear before the second month. If the programme is longer than six months, there should be short-term wins visible to staff approximately every six to eight weeks if they are to be effective.

2. *What type of change programme is it?* The nature of the change programme will play a part in deciding what constitutes an appropriate short-term win. For example, if we consider the case study at the beginning of the chapter, the fact that the change programme was very people-centric meant that key successes in the project itself acted as a key short-term win. If, on the other hand, you were looking at an acquisition programme, the nature of the short-term win is understandably different. Consider the effects of the change programme on individuals and teams in considering what best to utilise as a motivator.

3. *What type of people make up your team?* Think about the types of people working in your team. If you are a departmental manager, you will be thinking of the people in your department. If you are a member of the leadership team in your company, however, you need to try to get a broader picture of the people working for your company as an organisational community. Some questions that are appropriate here are:

   • Are they predominantly young and looking for quick wins and immediate responses?

   • Are they older and more interested in job security?

- Are there a number that are closer to retirement age who may be considering early retirement?

- Are they people who have been in the same job for a long time, or is this a new team?

- Do you operate in a sector where people's roles are quite established, or is this a more dynamic environment where the workforce is more used to moving jobs?

4. *What is important to them?* Having considered what sorts of people make up your team, you need to think about what may be important to them. At this stage you would need to start asking yourself questions about the personality types and mind-sets of the people you have been thinking about in question 3. The sorts of questions that you would be considering would be:

- Are they the type of people who are risk averse, or are they ambitious?

- Are they eager to encompass change?

- What are the key personality types of the people in the team?

- Is financial reward central?

- Is security more important?

- What about formal recognition within the company?

- What about the chance to grow within the company or learn new skills – could this be important?

Depending on your role within the company, these can be some of the most difficult questions for you as an Asperger leader to answer. One of the keys to being successful here is to remember that you do not necessarily have to do this all yourself. If you have a human resources department, make use of their skills. Ask them to prepare a report for you outlining their knowledge of the workforce, covering the sorts of questions outlined above.

If you do not have access to a human resources department, you could consider delegating this to a direct report of yours. However, I need to emphasise that if you decide to do this, you need to be very careful in communicating the reasons for you asking the questions. Asking for that sort of information automatically alerts people that 'something is coming' and it tends to be human nature to consider the worst scenario. Make it clear that you want to create a profile of the organisation so that you can develop an appropriate motivation system for them. If you are delegating this, be aware of the fact that you will need to be very transparent with your people about what you are doing. I do not recommend that you delegate this if you have yet to announce that a change programme is coming.

If you are unable to get the assistance of your human resources team in drawing up this profile, the resources in Part 4 of the book should provide you with a little insight into how to assess the profile of your workforce.

Key types of short-term win

There are a number of types of short-term win that can be built into your change programme. What is important for you to recognise is which of these would be most appropriate for both your change programme and the workforce profile you have identified. Let us have a look at some of the key types of short-term win.

Acknowledgement

Some people make the mistake of thinking that this is such a basic human motivator that it has no place in a change programme – or even in the workplace itself. In fact, the opposite is very often the case. Most significantly in the case of changes, acknowledgement is often a very powerful motivator for people going through the process.

For most of us with Asperger syndrome, acknowledgement is a skill that we have consciously had to learn. It does not come naturally to us constantly to reinforce to people that they are doing a good job. Our outlook would generally be along the following lines: 'Tracey has produced a good report. Tracey was recruited because we hire high-performing individuals. Tracey is a high performer. Therefore it is to be expected that her report is good.' In fact, we tend only to say something when the individual's performance is not what we expected – in this case, if the report was not good. We often assume that the people working with us know that we are happy with their work because we have not told them we are not. It goes back to our deficits in the area of theory of mind or mindblindness, as discussed in Chapter 2.

Most neurotypicals, however, do require some form of acknowledgement on a relatively regular basis. Of course, we must not fall into the trap of thinking that this applies to *all* neurotypicals. That would be the same as saying that all the effects of Asperger syndrome we have discussed within this book apply to *everyone* with Asperger's – to the same degree. Everyone is different – be they neurotypical or Aspergerian – but there are some general tendencies that we can recognise. The need for acknowledgement is one of them.

Although you need to ensure that acknowledgement is given to everyone, you must also ensure that you adequately acknowledge people who need it the most. This can include people who are having a particularly difficult experience as a result of the change programme, or who generally find change difficult. The topic of working with people facing particular challenges is covered in Chapter 20.

Recognition within the company

We cover this element later in this chapter, under the section 'Recognising successes: Examining failures'. Sharing the successes of your people with senior management and within the company as a whole can be a very strong motivator for some people. Again, you need to know your people well enough to understand whether this will motivate or just embarrass them!

You also need to remember that recognition within the company can take different forms, from a good word or email from senior management, to an opportunity for promotion at the end of the programme. I would also emphasise that there are both individual and team-based incentives. You should be making use of both forms.

Personal time

When people have achieved something according to the change schedule, or have made a significant effort in a difficult area, one way to recognise this is to allow people to have some time off (or at least away from the project). Change programmes take different forms and have different constraints in respect of time and resources. But if you are in charge of a change initiative which allows you the flexibility to allow people to have some time off to themselves, this can be a very valuable asset.

Once again, this is very much dependent on the type of people you have working with you, since some people would be very disappointed if they were asked to tear themselves away from the change programme, whilst others may suspect that you were sending them home because they had done something wrong. Be very astute in how you award this motivator. I would recommend asking them whether this is something they would like. If they hesitate or appear concerned or disappointed, be prepared to make an alternative suggestion, making it clear that this is being given in recognition of their contribution.

Tangible benefits

In some cases, actual physical items are the best types of short-term win for the people concerned. An example of this is in the case study given previously, where tangible benefits were given to people in the form of new flex benefits which they could apply to receive. Another example – although on a totally different scale – would be where a departmental head decided to take his team for a meal in London due to the extra work that they have put into the change programme.

Reward schemes

This type of short-term win may seem to be the most obvious for some people, but I encourage you to think of it as the last option rather than the first. This is the financial reward element, and can include things such as cash bonuses for reaching deadlines, and incentives for exceeding targets.

The trouble with using reward as a form of short-term motivation is that people then start to see it as an entitlement as opposed to a reward. It becomes a part of the remuneration package, and people begin to take it for granted. Incentive schemes can be invaluable, but rather as longer-term incentives, or programme-completion incentives.

Cash recognition awards

Unlike a reward scheme, one-off cash awards for achievement on a project will not be taken for granted to the same extent as a formal incentive scheme. However, if they become too regular or awarded to widely, they will certainly lose the excitement that spontaneity creates. Therefore, it is recommended that this be used on a limited number of occasions, and if you are issuing it to key people in the team rather than everyone in the team, that you are able to justify your reasons for the award. Beware of being seen to be playing favourites.

The key elements of making short-term wins work within your change initiative can be summarised as follows:

- Think about what type of change programme it is to help you understand how people will be reacting.

- Take into account how long your change programme is when deciding how to build short-term wins into it.

- Make sure you know the type of people you are working with.

- Try to find out or envisage what may be important to them.

- Make sure your short-term wins are ultimately for everyone who contributes, not just some.

- Make sure the win awarded is appropriate to the people in the team and the type of project.

Providing opportunities for the team

If you have been involved in any way in the process of team-building, you will know that the development of a team takes time to move from a number of independent parties to a cohesive unit operating in comparative unity. It doesn't just happen – it takes effort and commitment from the team leader and the new members to make this change to their environment possible.

When we go through a change initiative, the stability of established teams disintegrates. It happens. It is not a reflection of how good or how bad a team you have. It occurs as a direct result of the reactions people tend to have to change, as discussed earlier in the book.

In establishing short-term wins, you need to ensure that your people are involved in the development of key objectives for the programme. This applies to team targets as well as individual ones.

Take the time to develop work for the team that includes some very clear and well-documented requirements for contributions from individuals within the team. Set specific team targets and link these to your short-term rewards, as discussed earlier. Make the teamwork requirements visible.

Possible negative reactions from your people

As with many initial stages of a change programme, there is the potential for negative reactions from your people when they are faced with additional work they feel is required by your insisting on teamwork. Some of the negative reactions include the following:

- Rebellion. People could complain that project plans and goal-setting exercises are a waste of time, and that you are going overboard on your project management.

- Team members actually struggle to work together, with a spirit of one-upmanship taking hold, whereby people want to get the better of others.

- The team tries to split into its individual components to get the work done, only coming together superficially to present results.

- The work just doesn't get done.

To avoid these types of reactions, it is important that you communicate with your employees about the challenges they may be experiencing as a team. Make it clear to them that change tends to create challenges for teamworking, and that this is not a reflection on them as a team, or on anyone as an individual.

Frequently, people find that teamwork is more challenging, and become stressed and lose confidence in the team. If they are made aware that this is something that does tend to happen in the change environment, people find it much easier to identify when this is starting to happen and to push through those artificial barriers to teamwork, and once more start working together.

You need to emphasise the importance of teamwork in the success of the change programme, not only so that the work gets done, but also so that the people who work with you work through the change together as a unit.

Ultimately, you need to ensure that you are firm about the teamwork requirements for the change programme, but that you display empathy and openness to listening to any challenges that individuals in your team may be facing as a result of that requirement.

Leading by example: Being alert to your own teamwork challenges

I have detailed above the importance of teamwork to ensure the success of the change programme, and the necessity to communicate to your people the requirement that they work together as a team, despite any challenges they may be experiencing. I think it is very important at this point to highlight one of the most essential considerations for motivating your teams in this respect. This is the fact that you need to lead by example.

As people with Asperger syndrome, we often find that when things start to get stressful for us, we have a propensity to withdraw from others. Temporary withdrawal is generally one of our most successful coping strategies. As we come under pressure and feel an overload or shutdown approaching, we make the decision to withdraw from others and find a place to recover. Sometimes, this can mean leaving the office for a few minutes, or going to the restroom for 15 minutes, or closing oneself in an office for an hour.

In general, these strategies can continue to work for us. However, the extent of our coping strategy's withdrawal from others can make a difference. As I said, it could be that your coping strategy is to remove yourself from the office for a period of time. If that involves regularly removing ourselves from the office and other people for five-minute intervals during the day, this is unlikely to create a problem. However, if our coping mechanism requires our withdrawing from others for periods of an hour at a time, this is likely to create a problem. People will see that, although you are encouraging them to continue working as a team despite any challenges, you yourself are withdrawing and working independently. This will make you appear to be a hypocrite, or someone who feels management is exempt from any changes. The same will happen if you tend to close yourself in your office for long periods of time – you are shutting people out when they need to be able to see you and communicate with you. Therefore, coping strategies may potentially need to be reviewed. I have covered this in Part 4 of the book, with some exercises and practical tools to help you make any adjustments to your coping strategies.

Recognising successes: Examining failures

So we have our team starting to put some significant effort into the change programme and into changing their way of working. We have been successful in achieving their buy-in to date, and we want to ensure that we retain that buy-in throughout the programme. What is the best way to achieve this?

The answer to that question goes all the way back to what we said to our people to obtain their buy-in. We would have told them that the change programme was something we were capable of achieving. We would have identified some of the key activities we needed to complete in order to achieve the required change as part of the process of creating and measuring objectives. So people know what they need to do to get there. What they need now is to know how *well* they are doing along the way.

What exactly should we be recognising?

Each individual or group should have had objectives set for them as part of the objective-setting session at the beginning of the change programme. Many of these are likely to be operational objectives that you will be able to measure and easily assess the completion of. However, when we speak about recognising achievements here, we are talking about more than just acknowledging when key components of the project plan are ticked off.

Let's detail this a little more by looking at a case study.

Case study: The small courier with big plans

Company X was a small courier service operating in the East of England. Up until last year, their operations were pretty standard for a small courier service, in that they received a telephone call from a client, they collected the parcel and they delivered it. Prices for the drop were set based on the distance to be travelled from pick-up to drop-off point.

Problems had started to develop in customer satisfaction due to the fact that couriers often arrived late at the client offices, without notification, and similarly arrived late at the drop-off point. Clients never knew with any degree of certainty when their parcels would actually be collected, and – once collected – when exactly they would be delivered.

Within the courier company itself, the Operations Manager was experiencing problems with his operations team as well. He had the dispatch team dealing with the clients, who felt that there were drivers within the team who were taking advantage of the current system and doing personal things during delivery runs; hence the delays. The drivers, on the other hand, felt that the delivery times quoted to clients by the dispatch team were unrealistic and did not take traffic into account. They were also annoyed by the fact that clients themselves often created delays by having collection items that were far larger than expected, resulting in the drivers spending a long time loading items onto their trucks and trying to find space. They complained that if the client was going to expect such a large collection, then two drivers should go through, since it was a health risk for one person to lift and pack such large items.

Positives of the current system were that there were no instances to date of parcels going missing, and only a handful of claims for damaged items.

Following a strategic session held off-site by the leadership team of the company, it was decided that the company would make a significant investment in respect of the business, by purchasing a new billing system and a specialised tracking system for the vans.

The main difference for the billing system was that it calculated the size and weight of the parcel, together with the actual mileage between pick-up and drop-off sites, and used this as part of the billing mileage calculation. Discussions were held with the finance and systems people to ensure that the new system did not increase prices for the standard delivery, but focused on increased prices for clients sending bulk packages or large items.

The key advantages of the tracking system was that each van could be tracked live via satellite and their position noted on an online tracking portal clients could access once the order had been processed. In that way, clients would be able to ascertain how far the van was from their site or the drop-off point. Since the online service also had a traffic advice interface, the client was also able to see the traffic en route.

The new systems were advised to the people in the company, and the change programme in respect of operations and systems was announced. Initially, both dispatch staff and drivers were not very happy about the system changes. The dispatch team felt that the new system would require additional work for them, and the drivers were annoyed that they were being 'tracked'. However, following meetings with individual managers and their teams, the positives of the proposed system for both the organisation and the employees were acknowledged and the project took off.

Within the first week of announcing the proposed changes, the leadership team communicated their new system to their existing client base, and also developed a marketing campaign going forward.

The IT department set up a project team together with the external software consultants, and the Operations Manager pulled together his dispatch and driver teams to agree objectives and changes coming.

David, the Operations Manager, was aware that the ultimate reward for the team in terms of the billing and tracking systems being in place and fully operational was likely to be quite a long way down the line, and until then there would be a lot of disruption and increased workload. To assist with disruptions, David put in place a series of short-term wins for the team, including such small things as having a day out with the team, having a dress-down day, and so forth.

But one of the key things that David did do to keep his team motivated was to share all of the successes with the team as they happened. For example, within weeks of management advising clients of the proposed change to systems, they had a large number of clients coming back to them to say that the proposed changes were an excellent suggestion and showed great insight on the part of the company. David shared this with his team as a success, and included them all in the client's definitions of 'the company'. Another example was when the tracking system was fitted a week ahead of schedule. Once again, David shared this with his team and celebrated with them as a key achievement in the process of moving to their new, improved company.

By the time the new systems were up and running, David's team was eager and excited to be fully utilising the system. David continued to provide feedback to the team on the success of the new system for quite a long time after the actual implementation had been completed, such as positive feedback from clients, increased revenue in respect of billings and a less stressful environment for the drivers and customer services teams.

By the end of the year it was agreed that the strategy to introduce a new operational system was an overwhelming success and that the investment made in the new systems should pay for itself in the next four years.

The above example shows us that the successes being recognised by the change leader were not only the completion of objectives set for the individuals or team. They also included successes of the project which affected clients, other departments and the company as a whole. For example, David took the time to celebrate the feedback the managers received from their clients. Many would see this as being a 'tick' for the leadership team rather than something for the employees, but David recognised that, by including his people, he gave them a far greater sense of being part of the changes taking place in the company. Even though they weren't directly involved in the decision to update the systems of the company, David made them feel as if they had played a part and therefore clients were complimenting their insight as well.

Why is it so important to acknowledge successes?

The previous case study reflects how recognising successes can radically change the mind-sets of people going through change.

We know that people going through a change to their routine and recognised way of doing things are always going to be resistant to that change. We know that better than anybody. It is seen as a deviation from the norm, an alteration to the 'normal' way of doing things, an aberration. Even when people eventually buy in to making the change a reality, in most cases they are still resistant to or even resentful of having to change.

When you as the change leader are able to go back to your team and say to them, 'Look everyone, this is working. The following positive outcome has been achieved, the way we said it would,' you are showing your people that the decision they made to give this change a try was the correct one. You are allowing your people to feel that the additional effort and energy they have expended as a result of this programme has been justified, and that results are beginning to be seen, no matter how slowly.

You will also find that once people begin to see the results of their efforts in the change programme, many of them will start to put more energy into it. If you see something working, you tend to feel far more inclined to see it through and play an active part in the transformation.

Sharing your people's successes

It is very important for you, as change leader, to ensure that you share the achievements of your team with the leadership of the company. Nothing demotivates an achieving team more than having those achievements hidden. Take the time to share with your organisation or the leadership team what has been achieved by your people. If you cannot identify tangible objectives that have been completed yet in terms of a project plan, celebrate their enthusiasm, their commitment, their insight. And make sure that your people know that you are valuing their contributions. After all, it will do no good whatsoever to share the successes of your people with the leadership of the company if your people never get to hear about it!

Similarly, as a company leader, make sure that any press releases, interviews or reports acknowledge the contribution and support of your people. Recognise them publically.

But remember this. Recognising success within your team is a matter of balance. Balance between celebrating success and flattery. You do not need to be seen as someone who is going over the top in respect of compliments to the extent that these become meaningless to the team. Make the compliments valid.

But what about failures?

Just as important as recognising successes is dealing with failures or problems. You would be very fortunate indeed if you were able to undertake a change programme with absolutely no difficulties at all. It is recognised by the majority of change managers that the nature of the programme will often result in the potential for failure or delay in certain areas. The key to a successful change project is to ensure that these are identified and addressed as soon as they arise.

If people believe that failures in the project are reflections of their own shortcomings, they will try their best to hide or 'fix-up' failures rather than coming forward and saying, 'This didn't work.'

For this reason, an important thing that you need to communicate to your people is that shortfalls do sometimes happen. It may not be what we expect, and certainly not what we would want to see, but they do sometimes happen. The key is to address the failure and see what went wrong so that it can be corrected and this time be a success.

You need to encourage members of your team to let you know as soon as possible if there is anything which appears to be going wrong, or some part of the change programme which just is not working. The next step is to encourage your team to sort problems out together. Examine the failure as a team and see if there is anything that you can – collectively – think of which will help overcome the hurdle.

Coming up with a solution to this problem can in itself be a reason to celebrate – it is another form of success for the team, since they have put their minds together to overcome a barrier and as a result have played a direct part in the ongoing success of the change initiative.

Chapter 19

Key Skill 7

Dealing with the Undercurrents

Earlier in the book we discussed the challenges faced by the organisation and the leader as a result of the resistance of people to change. This chapter is going to focus on dealing with some of the more negative side-effects of people's insecurities – rumour mills, hidden agendas and politics.

Perhaps in starting the discussion, it is important to remind ourselves that when we speak of undercurrents, we mean anomalous behaviour within the organisation that has arisen as a result of change being introduced. It can take a number of different forms, some of which are more serious than others:

- mumblings against the organisation

- mumblings against senior management

- mumblings against yourself

- mumblings against the team or department

- mumblings against individuals in the team or department

- mumblings against the change management team

- mumblings against an external change consultant

- explicit negative actions or attitudes against any person.

Buchanan and Badham (1999) discuss what they call turf game tactics, where they identify the following actions as well:

- Image building: This is where individuals seek to raise their image in the company by taking credit for other people's work, always being seen to be the one with the answers or by tactics such as selective sharing of information.

- Selective information sharing: Only passing on selective parts of the knowledge they receive or have, thereby ensuring that others struggle, or that the change programme is negatively affected.

- Scapegoating: This is where a person makes sure that others are consistently blamed for any shortfalls of their own.

- Formal alliances: This is where an individual agrees actions directly with key people rather than working through their team or manager, thereby creating informal coalitions with them.

- Networking: This is where an individual deliberately tries to develop relationships with those people they see as important in the company, thereby making themselves 'known'.

- Role manipulation: Here an individual takes advantage of their role to influence a programme or affect other people. For example, they could refuse a request for information based on it being 'against company policy' to provide it, and yet grant a similar request from an alliance due to 'special circumstances'.

As leaders with Asperger syndrome, we need to acknowledge that recognising these sorts of issues with our people can sometimes be daunting. I have yet to speak to any person with Asperger syndrome who has been able to say that office politics is something they understand or handle with ease! This is understandable, since a large part of being successful at dealing with politics in the office is to be politically sensitive yourself.

Political sensitivity as a management skill

Baddeley and James (1987) discuss the importance of political skills for managers. According to them, there are two dimensions to political sensitivity, namely how politically sensitive you are (referred to as Reading Skills) and how you are able to put your emotions aside and make ethical decisions (referred to as Carrying Skills). Baddeley and James identified four types of manager as a result of this and used analogies of the Fox, the Donkey, the Owl and the Sheep to describe them (Figure 19.1).

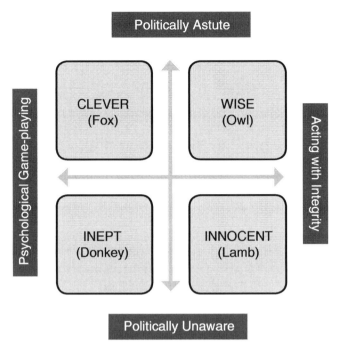

Figure 19.1 Political sensitivity of managers
(adapted from Baddeley and James 1987)

As mentioned, the two dimensions in this model are Reading and Carrying. Reading (as measured along the vertical axis of Figure 19.1) reflects an individual's ability to recognise the hidden, unwritten rules and ways of working in an organisation, underpinning the more formal and obvious rules and behaviour. Baddeley and James also note that it includes the ability to gather intelligence in respect of these areas and to act on them appropriately. Carrying (as measured along the horizontal axis of Figure 19.1) reflects an individual's ability to separate their emotions from the situation and to focus on the task rather than protecting their own feelings or interests.

If we examine the resulting quadrants of Figure 19.1, the four characteristic types of manager can be defined as follows.

The Clever Manager

The Clever Manager is politically astute, and therefore understands the undercurrents and particular situational circumstances well. However, they are also uncertain of themselves or their role in the change, and consequently can potentially engage in controlling and manipulative behaviours to attempt to strengthen their position.

Typical 'clever' behaviours suggested by Baddeley and James include:

- interested in power and in associating with the focus of power

- unprincipled, inner goal oriented, not ethical

- wants to be seen as powerful

- thinks before speaking, aggressive but well masked, charming manner

- doesn't display feelings spontaneously

- asks 'What information do *I* have? What information do *I* need?'

- checks gossip, rumour, is aware of others' viewpoints

- sees realities, knows how the formal processes work

- basically insecure, but well defended

- always leaves jobs before mistakes are discovered

- manipulates situations so as to appear never to make mistakes

- can make procedures work for them

- knows how the formal and information organisation works

- gets support, good at ingratiation, bargains, manipulates

- likes games involving winners and losers

- can recognise and exploit key weaknesses in allies and opponents.

Things Clever Managers are most likely to say include:

- 'Leave it to me, I'll have a word with him, he's out of touch.' [*Acts as gatekeeper of information; implies manager/colleague is out of touch*]

- 'I think it would be unwise for me to take this one, it's very delicate. How about you – you know how good you are.' [*Manipulates other person to take unfavourable task by false compliment*]

- 'I have discussed this very thoroughly and we were united in this.' [*Implies team decision making when this hasn't actually taken place*]

- 'I share some of his/her feelings on this matter, if not quite so passionately.' [*Undermines other employee by implying they are over-emotional*]

The Inept Manager

The Inept Manager does not read the political situation very well, and additionally is uncertain of themselves and their abilities. As a result, they tend to get defensive, trying to protect themselves from situations and behaviours they do not understand.

Typical 'inept' behaviours suggested by Baddeley and James include:

- not skilled interpersonally
- unprincipled
- hates to be ignored, likes to associate with authority
- inner-goal oriented
- doesn't recognise 'direction', doesn't appreciate political purpose
- plays psychological games but doesn't read those of others
- predisposed to projection, attribution and paranoia
- makes judgements/decisions based on feelings rather than knowledge of the bureaucracy or organisational procedures
- not ethical
- interpersonally inept at making alliances/coalitions
- tends to say 'Shall we take a vote?' in the wrong settings
- doesn't listen to others
- tries hard to be nice but doesn't know how
- sees things as either/or
- not tuned to the grapevine
- given to clichés – 'you know me', 'with due respect'.

Things Inept Managers are most likely to say include:

- 'Let's decide what we want and make it look like it's what they want.'
- 'Well, we all know how he got his job, don't we?'
- 'If the chairman wants to come to the meeting, we'll just have to tell him he can't.'

The Wise Manager

The Wise Manager is both confident in their role and abilities, as well as politically astute. As a result, they are more willing to be risk-takers, yet ensure they make ethical decisions.

Typical 'wise' behaviours include:

- aware of purpose
- interested in direction in association with power and purpose
- can cope with being disliked, good interpersonal skills
- personal values/ethics, thinks before speaking, assertive, tactful, emotionally literate, plans actions, checks gossip/rumour
- excellent listener, is aware of others' viewpoints
- takes account of other people's personality
- sees realities, knows how the formal processes work
- non-defensive, learns from mistakes, reflects on events
- can make procedures work for them
- sense of loyalty
- capacity for friendship
- knows the formal and information organisation
- open, shares information
- in tune with the grapevine
- recognises who knows, who cares, who can
- gets support
- negotiates/cooperates
- likes win–win situations.

Things Wise Managers are most likely to say include:

- 'How are *we* going to get this sorted out?'
- 'I wonder what's lying behind these ideas?'
- 'Let's look at the ways we can speed this up and get over the difficulties.'
- 'Let me make sure I understand what you're asking for.'
- 'I don't think I've been understanding you, can I have another go?'

The Innocent Manager

The Innocent Manager is confident in their own abilities and can act without being emotional or defensive. They are able to act ethically and in the interests of the programme. However, they are not skilled at reading the political situation or environment and can misinterpret situations or people's behaviours.

Typical 'innocent' behaviours include:

- principled, ethical
- tends to rely on authority
- doesn't appreciate political purpose
- doesn't network, doesn't know how to get support
- listens but doesn't hear underlying message
- sticks to ethical, organisational and professional rules
- understands content but not process of procedures
- exaggerated respect for rationality
- literal
- believes you are powerful if you are right
- doesn't recognise double messages
- sense of loyalty
- capacity for friendship
- open, shares information
- sees things as either/or.

Things Innocent Managers are most likely to say include:

- 'Could we get on with the main task of this meeting?'
- 'Well, in strict hierarchical terms, I think it's X's decision.'
- 'If only they would tell us exactly what they really want, we could get on with it.'
- '…in my professional opinion…'

Many of us will recognise that most Asperger leaders tend to fall into the category identified by low political awareness but high integrity, namely what is termed an Innocent Manager.

According to Baddeley and James, Inept or Innocent Managers tend not to make very good change agents. Understandably, they feel that the optimal manager for change is the Wise Manager. In order for us to move from being Innocent Managers to Wise Managers, all we need to do is to become more politically astute. This does not mean we need to become experts in office politics. What it means is that we need to be able to recognise some of the challenging behaviours identified above, and understand how to handle them.

In this chapter and the next one, I hope to give you some insights into both recognising and dealing with disruptive or challenging behaviour in your team or organisation. By doing so, we will be making the essential move from Innocent Manager to Wise one.

Now would be a good time for you to undertake the first part of Toolkit Exercise 4 in Part 4 of the book before returning to this point. This exercise will allow you the opportunity to assess how well you recognise potentially disruptive behaviour within meetings.

Recognising discontent versus rumours/negative vibes

Before we decide on a course of action to address any undercurrent manifestations, you need to decide whether what you are witnessing in people is true discontent or whether we are just witnessing someone who wants to create negative vibes in the company by generating rumours.

So let us ask ourselves two questions: first, what are the key differences between someone who is truly discontented and someone who is creating bad vibes as a negative reaction to the change; and second, how do we recognise them?

Someone can be described as discontented at work if they have something tangible occurring in their job which causes them to feel uncomfortable or stressed. Let me rephrase – this is when discomfort or stress is caused by an event or events that can be specifically identified, and which – once removed – should lead to the person no longer being discontented.

People who create bad vibes and initiate rumours are generally those who are having a negative reaction to a change programme, not due to some specific element of it, but purely due to the fact that it is happening. In short, people in this latter category tend to be venting their frustration at the change programme, the company, the situation, rather than feeling discontented because of one particular event. Another important distinction is that once the stressor for a discontented person is removed, they cease to be discontented. However, even if specific elements of a change programme affecting a person in the latter category are removed, they tend to continue to complain and stir.

This is an important distinction, because the way to deal with people who are discontented at work is very different from the way to handle people who are creating rumours and being trouble-makers in the workplace.

Typically, you will find that people who are genuinely discontented in the workplace will speak out about their situation or concerns in a broader forum, such as a team meeting, or they will bring it up directly with a trusted leader or manager. Alternatively, they may become introverted or quiet, seeming just to put their heads down and get on with things in the background.

People who are stirrers, on the contrary, tend to gossip behind closed doors and in small groups. They seem to be very skilled at getting other people worked up and discontented. Ironically, these people who have been influenced by the 'stirrer' may then speak out in a team meeting or to a manager, since they are now genuinely discontented as a result of the comments made to them.

Another characteristic of a 'rumour-monger' is that they will tend to deny any comments made, and very often will also deny even being disgruntled about the situation at all!

How to address the situation

Potentially, the easier situation to deal with is where an individual is genuinely discontented without having been stirred up by rumours. That may sound like a surprising thing to say, but it is far simpler to deal with a person who feels that they have a valid complaint and is willing to talk about it, as opposed to someone who wants to let everyone in the company know they are annoyed – except you. So first you will need to establish which situation you are dealing with.

Speak to the individual directly and determine whether the reason for their attitude is a result of something that has happened to them directly, or whether it is as a result of a rumour or some gossip propagated by someone else. If it is a genuine issue as opposed to a rumour, you will need to deal with this directly. However, if their discontent is as a result of the comments made by someone else, it is important that you advise the individual that what has been relayed to them is false information, and that you will be speaking directly to whoever spoke to them. You will need to try to reassure the individual that the rumour is a false one (I am, of course, assuming that it is a false rumour).

DEALING WITH THE PERSON GENERATING RUMOURS

Once you know that an individual has been spreading rumours or gossiping, it is essential that you speak to them directly. Depending on the climate in your company and whether the person concerned has a history of spreading rumours, this can either be done formally or informally. If it needs to be done formally, I strongly recommend that you speak to your human resources adviser first to ensure that you are following correct disciplinary procedures for the company.

However, in the majority of cases this will be an informal discussion you have with a member of your team. This is the approach I am describing below. For the pure sake of clarity of reading, I will from this point on refer to the person who is spreading rumours as 'the Stirrer'.

The first step is to confront the Stirrer. Tell them that you have been advised that they have been talking about the change programme (it is probably unwise to accuse them of spreading rumours), and sharing details that were not actually correct. Ask them to explain why.

As mentioned earlier, most people who are rumour spreaders tend to deny doing so; therefore it may be worthwhile confirming with the person who spoke to you that you will be sharing his or her name when you speak to the Stirrer. Whether or not the Stirrer acknowledges what they have said or done, it is important to make it clear that gossiping and spreading rumours is unacceptable, especially now.

Later on it is also useful to have a team meeting where the topic of undercurrents can be raised and the same message given to everyone. This needs to be presented from the perspective of your being concerned that perhaps other people have been spreading false information *to* your team, rather than implying that they are the ones doing the stirring. Explain to them that you find this unacceptable, and that if anyone appears to be trying to cause unrest, to let you know as soon as possible so that you can deal with it.

Always encourage your team to be open and to communicate any problems to you. In that way the potential for new problems arising is greatly lessened.

DEALING WITH A PERSON WHO HAS BEEN TARGETED

As mentioned, one of the ways that undercurrents can manifest is by an individual being targeted within the team or department. This could be an individual member of the team, it could be an external consultant, or it could be an internal change agent.

What do we mean by an individual being targeted? Well, a Stirrer will tend to make this person the focus of their rumours. They will imply that the person has had special favours, was part of the team that campaigned for the change, or is trying to get the best job after the change programme by walking over people. Whatever the Stirrer implies, he or she will make certain that this information is then spread around the department or organisation, and little by little the individual being targeted will become more and more isolated or shunned.

From an organisational perspective, this is a good example of bullying in the workplace. It doesn't have to be physical force. Bullying can – and does – take the form of isolation and rejection as well.

If you find out that there is an individual who has been targeted by a Stirrer, the first step is to confront the Stirrer, as mentioned above, although it is likely that this process is going to be more formal than the previous situation described. It is also worthwhile speaking to the person who has been the victim of targeting. Sometimes people are aware of the fact that they have been targeted, and deal with it accordingly. Others do not realise what is happening and feel that this is the result of something that they have been doing wrong. Confidence can suffer significantly in this scenario.

It is also important for you take the opportunity to speak to your team about what has been happening. They need to be made aware that individual targeting has been taking place, and that this is unacceptable. It is also important to emphasise that the reason for the targeting was invalid – that it was a case of false rumours or gossiping.

Typically this is done in a general way so that no fingers are pointed at any one person. No one wants the fact that they were targeted highlighted to the team. If members of your team have been giving someone the cold shoulder due to comments made by someone else, they will realise who you are talking about without having to be told.

However, as in many other situations, prevention is better than cure. So how do you avoid the situation where rumours are rife, people are being targeted and there is a general feeling of mistrust and discontent in the team as a direct result of a Stirrer?

Avoiding the undercurrent trap

The most important way of ensuring that the undercurrent trap doesn't snap shut in your department or team is through open and regular communication. I am sure you have heard it said often enough, but communication truly is key.

Make sure that you have regular communication sessions with your team to update them all on what is really happening in the change programme. If you haven't done so, I do recommend that you read Chapter 14 on communication, because it is a very important topic.

Make sure that people get the opportunity to ask you questions, and that if you have heard any rumours yourself that you address them in this forum.

People need to feel free to open up and speak without fear of repercussions. As ever, communication in both directions is very important. It is not just a case of you communicating information to your people, although this is still just as important. It is also essential for you to be the recipient of communication and information from your people as well, whether that is explicitly or implicitly.

Information reaches us either directly as a result of our teams speaking to us, sending us memos, emailing us, and so forth. This is the essential explicit communication that is referred to above. However, there is also another layer of communication that takes place between ourselves and our people. This is the informal communication of gestures and body language, innuendos and indirect references. This is the implicit communication that plays such an important role in our human communication process, and the area that can present us with the greatest challenge.

Think about someone working in your team who we will name Bill. Bill by nature is a bubbly, cheerful and enthusiastic individual who usually gives 100 per cent to his job. However, you notice that over the last two weeks he has become more introverted, is not as jovial as he usually is and is arriving and leaving work on the dot of starting and finishing times. Even though Bill hasn't come to you to tell you that he is unhappy about something, his body language and behaviour should be a very apparent signal to you that something isn't right.

During a change programme it is more important than ever to tune into the 'vibes' given off by your people. Get to know them. Make sure you can recognise when their behaviours change. This will also help you to identify any people who are struggling with the change – perhaps more than others. Part 4 of the book includes an exercise in the area of dealing with disruptions in meetings, a situation you may find arising when potentially disruptive behaviours arise.

Now would be a good time to go back to Toolkit Exercise 4 in Part 4 of the book, and to complete the final three parts of the exercise.

How to recognise your people's behaviours and some non-verbal indicators of stress are covered in the next chapter.

Chapter 20

Key Skill 8

Acknowledging Individuals Facing Challenges

Irrespective of how well we communicate change programmes to the group or team, it needs to be remembered that people are individuals, and not everyone is going to react to change in the same way. As a leader of people, it is important for you to be able to identify those of them who are struggling with the change programmes, and to work with them to try to overcome their problems.

The first step to being able to do this effectively is to recognise when individuals are starting to display signs of stress in order to then understand what is challenging them, with the ultimate objective of helping them with that difficulty. In dealing with any individual struggling with change, we initially need to be able to recognise that there is a problem. For those of us with Asperger syndrome, it is not always so easy for us to recognise the body language associated with people becoming stressed or trying to hide things from us. For this reason I am going to spend some time covering some of the body language associated with stress.

Ways to recognise stress, discomfort and deception

You may well be wondering why I have included the recognition of deception as part of this section. I think it is important to understand that when I speak of deception in the context of change, I do not mean that I feel people are out to deliberately lie or deceive you. However, when people feel under threat, they may feel that they need to conceal any difficulties they are experiencing, or at least hide them from you. They will probably feel that a failure to do so may put their job or future career in the company at risk. Therefore, they are likely to try to avoid certain issues, talk 'around' issues and sometimes even lie to hide what they may perceive as a shortcoming on their side.

I have read a number of books on understanding body language and – through trial and error over the years – have learnt which of these appear to be most accurate. What follows is a summary of some of the key behaviours and mannerisms associated with stress and deception that I believe may be helpful for you to recognise. This is not intended to be a comprehensive guide to reading body language, since this is a very broad and diverse area, but it will help you to be able to recognise the behaviours most commonly displayed.

As a starting point, let me highlight an important consideration for you as you apply this to your own organisation. Recognising the behaviour of people experiencing stress requires – by default – that you actually observe them. There are two things to keep in mind whilst you do this. First, observation needs to be done informally. If people notice that you are staring at them, always making notes about their behaviour or looking at them 'in a funny way', they are likely to become defensive and even more stressed. It is also likely that they will work harder to hide any issues they have. Similarly, if you are going to observe people informally, you cannot tell them that you are going to be doing so. If someone knows that you are going to be keeping an eye on them, they are also going to work additionally hard to hide their feelings, and may actually artificially change their behaviours when you are around, making it harder for you to identify problems. Walters (2000) suggests a number of considerations to assist in your observations:

- Be familiar with how the individual normally behaves. You can only observe changes in behaviour if you know how they normally act.

- Notice when behaviour changes or normal behaviour stops – what is being discussed at the time, what is being undertaken? This can give you an indication of what is causing the stress.

- Look to see if the individual acts consistently in future discussions of this topic, or in undertaking the same tasks.

- Look for clusters of verbal and non-verbal behaviour (discussed below) rather than one-off changes. Everyone displays unusual behaviour every now and then. What we are looking for is consistently unusual behaviour.

- Be open-minded about their behaviour – as I emphasise later, the causes of their reactions may not be related to the change itself or an indication of deception.

Walters (2000) identifies four channels that give away lies or attempts to hide things. These are body language, voice quality, speech quality and micro-expressions. Navarro and Karlins (2008) also talk about what they call pacifiers – behaviours we undertake to comfort ourselves.

Body language

A number of people have written on this topic, and I can recommend a number of good books (Ekman 2003; Jaskolka 2011; Navarro and Karlins 2008; Pease and Pease 2006; Vrij 2000). However, what we need to keep in mind when considering body language indicating that a person is under stress or potentially being deceptive is that context is key. What follows is intended as a guide for you, not a definitive method of determining whether a person is being deceitful. Remember that people have issues outside the workplace. An individual could be displaying all the signals of stress and withholding information, but this could be because of a personal situation at home rather than directly caused by your change programme.

The essential point is that you use this information to identify people who appear to be experiencing a challenge, and with whom it would be worthwhile speaking or offering encouragement to. Your actions need to be determined as a result of your conversations with them, not purely your interpretation of their body language.

Table 20.1 provides a breakdown of some of the key indicators of stress or dissent, as indicated by mannerisms from various parts of the body. However, I emphasise that these are considered signals in respect of neurotypical behaviour. I am certain many of you will agree that, for us, many of these 'indicators of stress or deception' are part of our day-to-day mannerisms. Therefore, do not be too prescriptive in respect of application: use these as indicators, not definitive signs.

Table 20.1 Common bodily indicators of tension, dissent or deception

Part of body	Mannerism
Head	Stiff, little movement, few expressions, head movements contrary to what is being said (e.g. nodding when disagreeing)
Face	Frowning, blushing, rapid blinking, knitting eyebrows, light sweating, either lack of eye contact (compared to normal) or too much eye contact (overcompensation)
Mouth	Covering the mouth, touching, rubbing or scratching the chin, biting the lip, biting nails
Arms	Crossed, one arm crossed over chest and hand holding other arm tightly

Fingers	Tapping, exaggerated movement or tightly clenched
Hands	Clenched, hidden (under arms, in pockets, under table), one clenched over other
Body	Tense shoulders, hunched shoulders, shrugging
Legs	Foot tapping, twitching, jerking; when standing, shifting frequently from one leg to another whilst body tense or arms crossed
Overall posture	Leaning backwards when in conversation with you, shifting frequently in seat, twitching or fidgeting

Table 20.1 indicates just how many types of body language can be observed, and how some can appear contradictory. What is important is for you to be able to notice when an individual you work with starts displaying clusters of these behaviours on a regular basis. Again, if you see this happening, do not assume that this means the person is lying to you. It could just indicate tension or a reaction to stress, either in the workplace or at home.

Voice quality

When an individual is stressed, their voice quality can suffer. This means that the pitch of their voice may either be raised or lowered, volume may increase or decrease, and the rate at which they speak could either increase or decrease. Examples could be that a person starts to speak really quickly, to the point where you have to tell them to slow down, or where an individual starts speaking quite softly in meetings when they normally are very audible. This is where it is important for you to know the individual's usual voice quality. You are unlikely to notice changes if you are not familiar with how they normally speak.

Speech quality

By speech quality I mean that an individual could start to stutter, pause or hesitate more than usual, correct him- or herself more often, stammer, mutter, or start interrupting their speech with sighs or nervous laughter. They could also do things like covering their mouth when they are speaking, rubbing their forehead or scratching their neck during their speech.

Micro-expressions

Micro-expressions (also known as micro-gestures) are small bodily movements that occur when someone is trying hard to suppress signs of something;

for example, if someone is trying not to act surprised by some news, or trying not to appear annoyed. Micro-expressions are very difficult to see, and are generally the kind of thing people would only really notice if they had the opportunity to review an individual's reaction in slow motion. I am not suggesting in this book that you need to take account of micro-expressions, since I believe that we have enough of a challenge recognising what I would refer to as 'macro-expressions'! This is just provided for your information.

Pacifiers

Many of us with Asperger syndrome are familiar with certain bodily actions we take to comfort ourselves. I have learnt, since being diagnosed, that this is referred to as 'stimming'. We will undertake a physical activity – such as hand flapping, tapping parts of our heads, tapping our feet, and so on – in a way that allows us to focus our attention enough to bring a potential overload situation under control. As an example, when I was in a stressful situation that made me feel as if I was becoming overwhelmed, I used to start tapping my forehead with my finger to provide an external focus. I did not actually realise I was doing this until someone I was consulting with at the time started to mimic me whenever I began to do it. It was only then that I realised what I was doing and how distracting this was for the other person, and determined to find a less 'visible' way to handle stress.

Pacifiers can be thought of as the neurotypical version of stimming. They are gestures people use to comfort themselves, and they vary according to the individual. Again, it would be useful for you to be able to have an idea of what individuals you work with do in a normal situation. What is their normal 'comforting' behaviour? Some may have none under normal circumstances, but others may have regular pacifier behaviours that they use on a regular basis. For example, an individual may regularly play with their hair. This is something you would discount as unusual pacifier behaviour for that person. However, if this was not something they usually did, you should be paying more attention to it.

Navarro and Karlins (2008) mention a number of common pacifier behaviours. Some of these are:

- rubbing chin, cheek or face
- touching or rubbing the neck
- rubbing or touching the forehead
- playing with a necklace or tie

- playing with clothing – especially shirt-collar or sleeves

- rubbing legs with the palms of hands

- chewing lips, licking lips

- playing with objects

- playing with hair.

If you feel it would be worthwhile supplementing the above information with some visual information, I can recommend a book by Anna Jaskolka (2011) called *The Picture Book of Body Language: The Only Language in Which People Can't Lie*. This contains a lot of visual information, not only for the work situation, but certainly covering some of the areas I have discussed above. As far as the work situation goes, I would recommend the book by Navarro and Karlins (2008) which has a number of very useful photographic examples.

Deception by omission

Another important phenomenon to consider is what is called deception by omission. Here, a person is being deceptive – not by outwardly lying, but by failing to disclose information. An example of this could be where you ask one of your direct reports whether they have completed a report, the deadline for which has now passed. The employee responds as follows: 'Yes, that really was a tight deadline, and there was so much more to the report than I realised. It is a good thing that we had the additional resources to ensure we covered everything we needed to, or it would never have been able to be completed on time.'

If this was the response your employee gave you, it would be very easy for you to assume that they were confirming to you that the report had been completed. However, if we actually analyse what was said in more detail, you will realise that the employee never actually confirmed that the report was completed. What he confirmed were the following points:

- The deadline was very tight.

- There was more to the report than he had anticipated.

- He needed the additional resources.

- If he did not have the additional resources, there was no possibility of the report being completed on time.

However, he does not actually say, 'Yes, I completed the report on time.' We assume that he is implying this from the final point above, but just because he could never have completed the report on time without additional resources, this does not confirm he did complete it with them either.

This highlights a very important element of your communication with the people you are working with. Make certain that any questions you ask are clear and straightforward, and that the replies you get from them are definitive and unambiguous. Using the above example, on receiving the response we did, it would be appropriate for you to then revert to: 'So, are you telling me that the report has actually been completed by the deadline?' Ensure that the answer is either a yes or a no response.

All the above should have provided you with a bit more insight into how to identify people potentially experiencing challenges with the change programme. In the next section we discuss how to help them.

Working with people experiencing challenges

In dealing with any individual struggling with change, the first step is to acknowledge that there is a reason for their reaction. Very often I have gone through to a client's offices only to hear the Chief Executive or Head of Department deride a number of employees for being trouble-makers or for having an attitude problem. This may well be the case, but it is your responsibility as leader to understand *why* they are acting the way they are. Terminating employees because they are having difficulty dealing with change is never the correct approach and reflects an ignorance of the underlying psychology of change.

In general, the reasons individuals struggle with change can be categorised under seven headings:

- reaction to loss of stability

- reaction to loss of self-control

- reaction to loss of power

- reaction to social losses

- survivor syndrome

- intrinsic rejection of change

- knee-jerk reaction to change.

These are discussed in detail below.

Reaction to loss of stability

This is a general reaction to change and the loss of stability that occurs as a result. Having discussed the change cycle earlier in the book, it should be readily recognised that this is the most common form of reaction to change.

People who experience this type of reaction are often those who have worked within one company for most of their careers, or who have held their current job for many years without significant change. Alternatively, they could be relatively young people who have come from a very stable home environment and as a result have never experienced significant disruptions. We also need to recognise that this will also include people who are particularly averse to changes to routine, acknowledging that this includes many like ourselves with autism or Asperger syndrome.

The best way to deal with individuals experiencing a negative reaction to the loss of stability is to spend time with them – either personally or through your human resources team – going through some of the principles of the change cycle. It is very easy to overlook the fact that change is very traumatic for people experiencing it for the first time, and that it is human nature to want to go back to what is comfortable rather than dive into the unknown.

Once the elementary change education has taken place, you should take the time to talk to people to ensure that they understand where in the process you are, and what happens next. Challenge them to get involved in the change programme itself, and share experiences of your own where you may have felt as insecure but were later able to enjoy a better work environment.

If possible, try to organise a mentor or coach for them, since there is no better aid in this situation than being able to share your experiences and challenges with someone who has been there and done that. Depending on your working relationship with the individual and whether or not you have disclosed your Asperger syndrome to them, you could very well be an appropriate mentor yourself.

Needless to say, this is one situation where your example will be invaluable. You need to show how you personally deal with any ambiguities and changes, thereby setting an example for them to incorporate into their own mind-set. Think about the exercises you did as part of Chapter 10 and how you could explain your coping strategies to someone else.

Reaction to loss of self-control

This is a reaction to the loss of self-control that occurs when systems, people or departments change around the individual, over which the individual has no control.

People feeling a loss of self-control are generally recognised as being those struggling to come to terms with no longer being able to work the way they used to, showing signs of insecurity over new ways of working, and generally rebelling against new systems or processes being forced on them. They are reflecting an intrinsic fear of being controlled by others and loss of freedom, and for some individuals this may be a lot stronger than for others. The following case study provides an example.

Case study: IT support reorganisation

David was a key IT support person working for a company based in Peterborough. He had worked in the company IT department for a number of years dealing with email and software problems for staff. His usual way of working had been to receive a phone call from an employee to notify him of a problem, during which time he would talk through the problem and steps necessary to resolve it with the employee. If the problem was more extensive, David would go and visit the employee concerned and fix the computer personally. As a result of the set-up, he was very much in control of his own work and had very little contact with anyone else in the IT department, which suited his personality. It wasn't that he was not social, but he preferred to mix with people within the business rather than just the IT community.

Last year an organisational redesign programme was initiated, focusing on the internal support functions. IT was identified as a key area for change. As a result of the diagnostics work done by the external consultants, it was decided that the IT function would be re-engineered into an IT support centre. All IT support staff, like David, were transferred to a call-centre-type environment, and assigned to teams of three. They were then trained as a team to receive any IT calls electronically and log them onto the IT support system. If the problem was more extensive, they were able to connect to the person's computer remotely and investigate the problem directly. There was no longer any need for the IT support team to go to employees or speak to them directly. It was also a requirement that follow-up calls were made to the employee by another member of the team to ensure that the work had been completed correctly and to the employee's satisfaction.

Needless to say, by the time we spoke with David, he was ready to leave the company. His manager had not recognised the challenge that this type of change would present to him, and the loss of both control and social contacts in his new role was almost overwhelming for him.

A review of the new organisational design, together with some development sessions for the IT Manager and an employee diagnostic survey, allowed us to revise the model originally designed only slightly to cater for that 20 per cent of the IT support employee population who were in the same situation as David. It was decided to rethink the IT support team model to make it a team of four with one dedicated IT customer support person. The role was defined as the person who liaised on a regular basis with all people who had received support through that team to ensure that the correct work had been done and to ensure that there were no ongoing problems. Not only did this revision to the original design have the effect of providing a more compatible role for David and those people in the department with similar profiles, but it also gained the IT function a recognition award from the business for customer service.

As the above case study shows, the way to address similar issues is very often to review the current situation with your people. Get to know your people. Understand what makes them tick. Be open in your communication so that even if you do not pick up exactly how they tick, they feel confident enough to be able to come and tell you themselves if something is creating a problem for them.

Reaction to loss of power

This is a reaction to the loss of power a person has to determine their own way of working or dealing with people in the organisation.

People experiencing a reaction to their loss of power are generally recognised by their tendency to become over-controlling in their work and working relationships, largely subconsciously. A good example of this is where a senior administrator within a department undergoing change starts to experience a reaction to loss of power and as a result becomes rather extreme in respect of who is allowed to access any reports on the main database of the department server, insisting that all requests are signed off by him- or herself.

This type of reaction to change can be very challenging in a team environment, especially where the rest of the team has encompassed the change, since the person caught up in his or her insecurities will be hindering the progress of the change programme, and creating tension by forcing people who had previously had the freedom to operate without restriction to submit to artificially created 'vetting' or authorisation processes.

Dealing with this requires you sitting down with the individual concerned and having a 'heart-to-heart'. As mentioned, in most cases people do not even realise how controlling they may have started to become. If they have realised it, they may attribute it to a need for control 'given the circumstances'. It is your responsibility to ensure that you can talk them through the logic behind the reason for their change in working style, and help them to see that just because they are in a transitional state due to a change programme it does not mean that they have lost their 'power' within the organisation, but that their environment is just altering.

It often assists to help people see how much insecurity their own actions are causing for the people affected by their over-controlling behaviour, since they will probably be able to identify with them and hence realise the need to change their own behaviour.

Reaction to social losses

This is a reaction to the loss of friendships or social relationships to which the person has become accustomed.

Although with many managers this is not really considered to be a critically important factor in a change programme, for neurotypicals in the workplace, social relationships define the working environment, and therefore a potential loss of a social network can be devastating for some of them. People reacting to this type of insecurity are often seen to be more emotional than usual and sometimes less accurate with their timekeeping as they try to fulfil their social needs elsewhere in the company or externally.

Addressing this can appear daunting, especially for us. Unfortunately, it generally needs to be addressed by a rather more firm approach than some of the others. Whilst it is important to show empathy to the individual concerned with regard to how they are feeling about potential loss of social relationships, it is also important to explain that they are in a business environment, and relationships here do tend to come and go. As one set of social relationships ends, so another begins.

Encourage the person to come and speak to you if they are feeling isolated or challenged, but at each meeting make sure that you do emphasise that their situation will change when they start to develop their new network of friends.

Ultimately, business must come before social relationships.

Survivor syndrome

A very real difficulty that some people may experience as a result of a change programme that involves a loss of jobs is that of survivor guilt. Noeleen Doherty (1997) describes this as survivor syndrome, whereby people feel overwhelmed with guilt for the fact that they have stayed in the company and kept their jobs whilst others (and possibly their friends) have lost theirs. The person often starts to feel that they are not worthy of having been selected to stay, that the management made a mistake in keeping them. As a result, their productivity will suffer, and they could subconsciously sabotage their work to try to prove that their feelings are correct and that they really were not worthy of staying on. Self-confidence suffers, and the individual begins to doubt their own decisions and the value of their contribution to the company.

Survivor guilt is a form of trauma, and it is often recognised that this is suffered by people who have survived an accident or incident where others have died. Despite this having a far less dramatic cause, the side-effects and behaviours are the same.

There are a number of ways to deal with individuals experiencing survivor guilt, some of which should actually be considered before your change programme begins. If you are going to be making people redundant, it is important that you consider such things as outplacement programmes to support people leaving the company to adjust and find new work. Sharing details of this programme with those who have remained in the company will help employees feel that their ex-colleagues are being treated fairly. In addition, make sure that the issues around how people are going to be feeling are actually covered as part of the change communication programme. Having counsellors available for people, or the opportunity to be referred to an independent counsellor sponsored by the company for a defined period, can also help.

However, a very significant part of this revolves around your just being there. You need to be able to talk to people, let them know that you care, that you are available to speak to, that you understand.

Intrinsic rejection of change

This is the inherent rejection of change or the unknown. Whilst every individual experiences this type of insecurity to some extent or another, there are some people who have a far more negative reaction to change than others. For them, the inherent rejection of any change is a very powerful, and often completely subconscious, reaction. This can be recognised in individuals having a generally negative attitude towards the change, no matter what the positive outcomes may be. It is probably fair to say that until we found ways to cope with some of our challenges, we fell into this category. It should be easier, therefore, for us to empathise with their reactions than most neurotypical leaders can.

For individuals struggling with this type of reaction, their focus is purely on change as a negative and unwanted interruption to their working life. They generally display one of two types of behaviour. The first one is that of fear and denial. Individuals get stressed when anything related to change is brought up and as a result try to ignore or avoid anything to do with it. The second type of behaviour is that of anger and stubborn rejection of change. People vigorously defend why things should remain as they are and very often refuse to make any conscious effort to adapt to changes taking place around them.

The best way to deal with individuals in this place is to invest some time in focusing on the positive results of the change. This will usually be a challenge in itself, since the individual will often counter with an array of reasons why the positives you have outlined are not actually positives, but negatives! Have one-to-one meetings with them, but be sure that you are not going over the positives again and again. They need to be outlined clearly once, as part of a motivational meeting, and made clear to the individual that these are the positives to aim for.

The unfortunate reality of this type of reaction to change is that people in this place often become so centred on rejecting anything related to the change that they become incapable of integrating with the new organisation. If this eventually happens, you will have no option but to let them leave, since they will act as an ongoing negative attitude within the company, shackled to the 'old way of doing things'.

Knee-jerk reaction to change

A knee-jerk reaction to change is where people have recently (or even not so recently – depending on the circumstances) been through a negative change experience. Examples of this would be where individuals have recently joined the company after having been made redundant from another company, or those who have survived a really difficult company acquisition process.

Often there is more of a challenge in recognising these individuals, since their behaviour may at times appear to be that of an individual with an inherent rejection of change, and at another time that of an individual struggling with the loss of social networks in the workplace.

That being said, the above display of alternating – if not erratic – behaviour is often what helps identify an individual experiencing this type of reaction. They often communicate a very negative message about the change programme, convinced that there will be a negative outcome, although this tends to be done via the rumour mill. Often they can appear to be panicking about the change programme and may become angry or emotional.

The best way to help these individuals is through patience and time. This is one of the few situations where a face-to-face meeting with the individual may have a negative effect, since – if the person has had a bad experience in the past – they may see being 'called into the boss's office' as something very negative, no matter what you have detailed as the purpose of the meeting, and this perception will doubtlessly colour the perception of the meeting from the employee's perspective.

A better strategy is to ensure that they are involved when your general communications are done, and perhaps that they are invited to be part of one of the project teams. Ensure that they are there when the positive messages are given, but also the negative, and make sure that you emphasise your intention to be transparent in respect of the change programme. If you are able to, partner them up in some activities with those individuals you know are positive and confident enough about the change programme not to be negatively influenced.

However, there must be a cut-off point identified by you in advance, after which time – if your employee has not changed his or her attitudes – you will need to have a conversation with them and explain how his or her negative attitude is affecting the environment. Be open about the fact that you know why they may be concerned, but explain that the change programme needs their support. Once again, you need to offer empathy to the person concerned, but still confront the negatives in his or her behaviour.

Leadership and loyalty

There is one last point that I would like to add to this chapter, and that concerns the concepts of leadership and loyalty.

Many leaders reading through this section may be struck by the amount of effort required from them in helping people to work through change when they are struggling. Some may feel that this is a waste of their time and an activity which should be undertaken by their HR people, if at all.

But the reality is that a large part of being a successful leader in a company is centred around offering your hand to those people struggling in the quicksands of fear and confusion. Some of the most successful leaders are acknowledged as being those who take the time to motivate their people and help them overcome the difficulties they are facing.

But why does helping people overcome their challenges result in the individual becoming such a success? It is because of the loyalty that they earn from their employees as a result.

This is best reflected in a comment I heard from an employee (Charlene) talking about her manager who had recently helped her to cope with the challenges of a change programme affecting her department, and which she had struggled with personally. At the time, her manager had invested a lot of time in helping Charlene to face her challenges, to the point of other staff wondering if the manager was overdoing it.

However, a year down the line, Charlene was a key strength in the department as a new change initiative was rolled out across the business, helping to make the department a role model for the rest of the business. When asked about her enthusiasm, Charlene commented, 'She [her manager] helped me out when I thought I wasn't going to make it and was thinking about leaving the business. She showed me her faith in me as an individual and helped me overcome my fears. She is a fantastic role-model and I would do anything for her. I just hope I can help the others in the business as much as she helped me.'

This point leads us to the discussion point of our next chapter – developing internal change agents.

Chapter 21

Key Skill 9

Developing Internal Change Agents

During change programmes, it is not unusual to find members of your team who appear to be handling the change better than others and to whom other team members turn for support. These individuals can end up being very influential in the change process, since they can both encourage those people in the department who are struggling, as well as take the lead on implementing changes in the department that assist in introducing a new way of working.

Identifying these individuals and developing them to become your internal change agents is both beneficial to the rest of the people in the team and essential for you to ensure that you continue to have the ongoing commitment of the team and the enthusiasm that can only be generated as a result of a mentor within the team. Your role as leader of change is to provide direction, motivation and enthusiasm to the whole organisation (or your whole division or department) rather than individually. Change agents within your team are those people who emulate what you are trying to introduce at a far more individual and personal level.

So how do you go about developing these internal change agents? In fact, how do you even go about identifying them?

Recognising people in the team who are change agents

One of the first ways in which you can identify an internal change agent is to have a look at those people in your team that other team members tend to confide in when they are facing challenges. Now, as leaders with Asperger syndrome, that is actually not as simple an observation as it would be for most neurotypicals. How do we know when someone is confiding in someone else? How do we know when this is positive rather than just focusing on the negatives of a change programme? It isn't easy to answer that question, because the answer really does depend a lot on the context within which all this happens. Within some organisations, it is considered a good thing for employees to discuss their concerns with one another; within others it is considered disruptive and totally inappropriate. The culture of your organisation will play a large part in how much of the 'social support' side of the workplace you actually get to see. On top of this, you – as an individual with Asperger syndrome – have your own level of ability to recognise social signals.

But there are ways to identify change agents, even if the environment you are in makes this harder for you.

One of the most obvious signals you can look out for is where one or two people tend to come to you to ask questions or raise concerns on behalf of their colleagues. There are two main ways that people do this. First, they could approach you, openly stating that someone has asked them to speak to you on their behalf. I refer to these people as Messengers. Alternatively, they could come to you and say they just wanted to bring something to your attention that they had noticed from the team as a whole, or indicate that a number of people have suggested/asked something, etc. I refer to these people as Advocates.

In general, it is the latter type of person, the Advocate, who is acting on behalf of the team. Whilst the Messenger bringing something to your attention on behalf of someone else certainly does show that they have been approached by a team member, the fact that this person has then told you who asked them to intercede indicates that the Messenger does not want to continue to be the intermediary – they are, effectively, just passing along a message.

In the case of the Advocate, the individual advises you of something on behalf of others in confidence. They have spoken to him or her, knowing that the Advocate will be the person who will keep their individual identity confidential, and act as the 'front guy' for the questions and answers.

Once you have identified that an individual appears to be acting as an Advocate, the next thing that you need to consider is whether they are representing the people to you with a positive mind-set or a negative one. What do I mean by this?

Toolkit Exercise 5 in Part 4 of the book provides you with a very practical exercise to help you understand the above. I recommend you turn to Toolkit Exercise 5 in Part 4 and complete this exercise before continuing with the rest of the chapter.

The exercise you have just completed in Part 4 of the book has the intention of clarifying what I mean by a positive versus a negative mind-set. This is crucially important in identifying potential change agents in your company. In the three conversations detailed in the exercise, Jake and Gina were both acting as Advocates for their colleagues. However, Jake's approach to the change was positive, and he was approaching you with a view to helping to resolve an issue that was surmountable. He was approaching you as an Advocate with a positive mind-set. Gina, on the other hand, was not coming to you in a supportive manner, but rather in an aggressive, threatening way – trying to force you to change your plans to suit the employees. She saw herself as one of 'them' rather than part of 'you as management'. Gina was approaching you as an Advocate with a negative mind-set.

If you notice that you have one or two people in your organisation or team who appear to be acting as positive Advocates for others, make sure that you make a connection with them. When they come to speak with you, take the time to ensure that you communicate back positive messages and an acknowledgement of their concerns. Thank the person for coming to speak to you, and encourage them to continue to do so. An important point here is that these are the people that your team turn to for encouragement and assistance in moving forward, so the more support they have in sharing information, the better for the organisation as a whole.

People who are genuine internal change agents are those who assist people when they are struggling, provide encouragement and seem to be able to come up with some solution when challenges arise.

You may also find yourself in the situation where you are the only person to whom people speak or confide, and whilst this may be a very good testament to your leadership skills, it does tell you that at present you do not have any strong internal change agents other than yourself. In this situation you will need to look at people who are perhaps moving in the direction of becoming internal change agents, even if they haven't actually reached their confidence peak yet. Again, these may be people who come up with the ideas, who appear to be supportive within the team, and who feed back concerns about the change to you – not necessarily on behalf of anyone in the team, but possibly as a result of observation.

Developing your internal change agents

It is certainly worthwhile investing some time and effort in developing your internal change agents. If your organisation has an internal training programme on change management, make sure that they attend it. Once you have completed the majority of the change programme, send them on an external programme for change leadership. This will help them to become successful leaders of your next change programme themselves.

Before you do any of this, however, make sure that you take the time to speak to them and explain that you have identified that they appear to be very strong change leaders, and that you would like to give them the opportunity to develop their skills. You may find that the individual really doesn't want to be developed into a change agent, and wants to give up the role on completion of the current change project. This is always a possibility which needs to be recognised. As leaders with Asperger's, most of us are aware that we have various degrees of mindblindness, as discussed previously, and that as a result we may unintentionally 'project' our own interpretation of what we think these individuals would like to do with their careers rather than understanding that they may not share our enthusiasm.

You may find that they have already had formal change management training in the past, and all they need is some mentorship and the opportunity to use their skills formally.

It goes back to making sure that you customise your actions for the individual, and are not too generic.

Encourage them to start coaching others

Having had the discussion and agreed some development for your budding change agent, the next step is to arrange for them to have the opportunity to start coaching others.

There is certainly no better way to encourage your change agents than to let them do some official coaching in that area with your full support. Being an internal change agent is something that people do, not only learn about. So make sure that you provide the opportunity for them to do what they appear to be talented in doing. Make them workstream leads for projects, give them special projects or add them to key committees.

If you have people in your team who are currently feeling overwhelmed or threatened by the change programme, sit with them and let them know that you are there to help them, and in order to do so you are going to let the 'internal change agent' spend some time with them to work with them on some of the challenging issues and see if together they can come up with a solution.

But what about the negative Advocates?

In this chapter I have largely focused on developing your positive Advocates into internal change agents. That does not mean, however, that the negative Advocates do not have a role to play. In fact, leaving them out can be extremely risky. However, their role would be somewhat different.

As a consultant, I have frequently been asked how I have been so successful in getting the buy-in of what management see as the pessimists in the company, such as the unions, the long-term employees and some employee representative groups. My response is simple – I include them. No matter what the change programme is, I believe it is essential for you to include members of the 'challenging' or negative groups in your programme management. Get those people who are negative Advocates involved in focus groups, or special projects, or communication teams. It is amazing the difference it can make to a challenging working relationship – such as that between a company with a very strong union – when you approach the union at the beginning of the change programme and openly invite them to take part. Apart from indicating to all parties that this is a reciprocal working party, it also emphasises management's intention to be transparent as far as possible, and to take the view of the employees seriously.

So you have identified your prospective internal change agents and have taken the necessary steps to encourage them to engage in their role. Very often, however, it is still necessary to bring in external change consultants to assist with the more technical aspects of the change initiative. As a leader with Asperger syndrome, you need to make sure that you build an appropriate relationship with them in order to make optimal use of their skills, as outlined in the following chapter.

Chapter 22

Key Skill 10

Working with External Consultants

I am going to open this chapter by covering two case studies each of which highlights a different challenge in respect of the utilisation of external consultants in the change process.

Case study: External change consultants – Scenario 1

Patrick Robertson sat in his office with the door closed. All he could think about was how he would much rather be at home than at the office – and that was a feeling he was not used to experiencing. Three months ago everything had appeared to be going so well with the new organisational restructuring project, and now it lay around his feet in tatters. What – WHAT? – had gone so terribly wrong?

The shadow of a person walking past his office caused Patrick to glance up, but they didn't stop at his door. Sighing, Patrick relaxed in his chair – disappointed that he had become so tense at the prospect of someone entering the office. How had all this started? It had all started with the appointment of Harold Davies, the specialist change consultant.

Three months ago a change project had been announced and communicated to staff. Patrick felt that it had been handled well – the Human Resources Manager was a competent lady who knew her stuff, and she had ensured that all the staff were well briefed and counselled where appropriate. But Patrick knew that in order to do a proper job in making this restructuring work, it was really important to bring in a professional.

It was at that time that he had been introduced to Harold Davies, a well-known change management consultant and professional speaker. When Harold had come through to the company to meet with him and review the potential project, Patrick had been quite awed at the man's technical knowledge in the area, as well as the aura of professionalism which he projected. If anything, Harold made Patrick feel as if this particular project may actually be quite simple for him – too simple in fact – and that he could lead them through it blindfolded. He had offered him the contract on the spot.

When Patrick had announced to the team that he had hired Harold to undertake the change programme, Lisa – his Human Resources Manager – had made the observation that Harold had not taken the time to meet with any of the other people he would be working with, or to give them at least some indication of how he intended to undertake the work.

Patrick had dismissed her comments as being superficial – after all, why did the consultant need to speak to the staff? He was confident that Harold would know how best to do the change programme – he was, after all, the specialist.

If he was honest, *that* was where the problems had started.

Patrick had never been a very hands-on manager, and so was very pleased to leave his specialist to 'get on with what he did best', as Harold himself put it. In fact, Patrick had been surprised to find that all he had been expected to do was to introduce Harold to the Leadership Team of the company, as well as advise him who would be reporting to him. Patrick did the necessary introductions (all members of the Leadership Team being very impressed with Harold) and introduced him to Lisa as being the key person with whom he would be working. And he had left them to get on with things.

Within a week, Lisa had come to speak to him about the situation with Harold. He remembered that she had been very concerned about the way Harold was introduced into the project and recalled that at the time he had dismissed her complaints as being made due to jealousy. He thought she was trying to undermine Harold because she had been expecting to be put in charge of the change programme. So he ignored her new concerns.

Patrick noticed that his team was starting to play less of a part in their meetings, and that nothing seemed to be happening as far as restructuring was concerned. On spending more time with some of his key team members, it became apparent that they did not think very much of this new consultant. Once again, Patrick thought that this was just a case of his team rebelling against having a specialist showing them how to do things properly.

But just to make sure, he called Harold in for a project update meeting. He had asked the consultant to go through the project plan and tell him where they were in the timetable. Harold breezed over the issue of the project plan, explaining that he did not operate according to strict project plans, but rather according to 'application'. Harold explained this concept so technically that Patrick hadn't even considered challenging him. Harold also explained that he did not formally manage any of the change work, but delegated this to the people who actually worked in the company – in this case Lisa.

The following week, Patrick called a project meeting with the change team. He was disappointed to hear that Harold was unable to join them, but apparently he had a meeting scheduled with the CEO. But his team wasn't disappointed. They had taken the opportunity to air a number of complaints about the change programme taking place, including the fact that Harold had never actually given them an action plan, and when Lisa had finally drawn up a project plan for them, Harold kept changing it at key points. The team acknowledged that Harold was certainly a 'guru' in respect of the theory of restructuring, but he didn't appear to know how to – or have an interest in being able to – apply this knowledge practically.

By now Patrick was starting to feel concerned. He realised that there appeared to be a lot of credibility to the concerns Lisa had raised right at the beginning, and it did appear as if the project was struggling to get going. Patrick determined to speak with Harold and get him to commit to Lisa's project plan once and for all, or explain his reasons for changing it. After all, surely something was better than nothing.

Patrick did meet with Harold, and advised him that they were going to follow Lisa's project plan. Harold didn't appear very happy with this, but since he was unable to provide any reasons not to go ahead, he agreed.

Within two more weeks, the improvement in the atmosphere in the company was becoming apparent – or so Patrick thought. He recalled the CEO calling him in one morning and telling him about the negative attitudes displayed so openly by so many. Patrick tried to explain that the restructuring project had taken a while to get off the ground, and that may have been a contributing factor, and tried to explain just how much attitudes were improving now that the project was under way.

'Ah yes,' the CEO had said, 'Harry mentioned to me that he was having his plans interfered with and this may be causing some problems. Seriously, Patrick, I want you to let Harry do what he does best – he is the expert here, after all, not you. I've already told him I would have a word with you. Given the way the programme has been off-track since you changed his project plans, wouldn't it be better just to let him run the programme without so much micromanagement?'

And so the deadly decline had started. Patrick had been forced to go back to his team and tell them that they would no longer be following Lisa's project plan, but would be following a new one that Harold would be pulling together. The disappointment had not only been palpable, it had also been very tangible. Five of the change team members had resigned, including Lisa, and the rest of the team appeared to lose motivation to do anything constructive. Harold's role became more and more of a personal adviser to the Leadership Team rather than the project leader of the change programme, and the Leadership Team considered the failure of the project his fault.

Patrick packed his briefcase and prepared to leave the office. It was early, but he didn't care any more. 'I wonder,' he mused as he left the building, 'would any of this nonsense have happened if I hadn't appointed an external consultant?'

Case study: External change consultants – Scenario 2

Mark Yin was an experienced Operations Director within the financial sector. He was acknowledged as a key contributor to many strategic conferences and was well respected within the industry. So when Paul Hodes was approached by Mark to undertake a potential change management project, Paul couldn't have been more excited.

Paul Hodes was a freelance change consultant specialising in large-scale change programmes within the financial sector. He had originally worked within financial services himself before deciding to go independent doing what he felt he did best – leading change.

Paul had been impressed by the interview and competency assessment which Mark had undertaken with him to ensure that he knew his stuff and would be able to drive the project. It was much better to know that the client understood the necessity for application and leadership of the change – it made it far easier when presenting challenging project plans.

Mark had taken the time to explain to Paul that the people were currently in a 'negative space', as he put it, due to a number of proposed changes that had never got off the ground. As a result, they were unlikely to be very positive and cooperative with this change project, but the programme needed to go ahead nevertheless. Paul had reassured Mark that he had been in similar situations – which he had – and explained that all he needed was an outward display of Mark's support for his role in the project and the authority to lead it.

After that Paul was introduced to Mark's team. They were a nice crowd, albeit a very suspicious and certainly very negative one. But that was what Paul had been expecting, given Mark's comments earlier. He determined to try to be a positive influence on the team, but to ensure that he met Mark's strict requirement of pushing the change through, 'no matter what'.

Paul arranged to meet with the team the first day that he was there, to give them an opportunity to ask him any questions they may have had, as well as for him to outline how he intended to start the project off and help them reach their objectives. He noticed immediately that the team was more than slightly dismissive of his ideas, and were very focused on business as usual rather than any of the changes which had been announced in the company. He ended the meeting by making arrangements to meet with each of them personally in order to go through their individual roles in the change project.

The individual meetings turned out to be very interesting. A large number of the team members were very determined not to disrupt business as usual, and saw Paul as making a nuisance of himself. Paul was interested to hear most of them comment on several occasions that they would 'speak to Mark about that', and he determined he should have another meeting with Mark to ensure that he had actually communicated that Paul did have the authority to run the project.

When Paul got together with Mark, he went through the project implementation plan he had developed together with Mark's team. Mark indicated that he was happy with the project plan, but emphasised that it was important that timescales did not slip. Paul raised his concerns about the commitment of the team to the change programme, and asked Mark whether it had been formally communicated that he was there to lead the change programme. Mark reassured Paul that there was no question over him having the authority to determine how things needed to be done during the change project, but said that he was aware that his team were not comfortable with the proposed changes. He undertook to speak to them individually to confirm that he supported Paul's project plan and encourage them to play an active role.

Paul continued with the change programme, but he still felt that the resistance to his leadership was interfering with the progress of the project itself. One day his instincts appeared to be proven correct as far as one of Mark's team was concerned. Dorian Smith was the IT Manager who was to play a key role in the implementation project. In the project meeting, Paul had asked for the status of the actions agreed at the last session. Dorian had stated that he hadn't actioned them. Paul questioned why, and was surprised to hear Dorian retort that he had been hired by Mark to run the IT department, not to help a 'temp' with some silly project. Paul clarified that he was not a 'temp' and that Dorian had been appointed to the change project by Mark, and therefore was required to play the game. He reiterated what Dorian's actions were and a new deadline for their completion, and advised him to get started.

Two days later Paul had his update meeting with Mark. Running through the progress to date, Paul mentioned the slight 'hiccup' experienced with Dorian, but reassured him that he had explained to Dorian that the project needed to go ahead and therefore he would need to undertake the agreed actions.

Paul was rather taken aback, though, when Mark then advised him that he, too, had spoken with Dorian, who had come through to him to complain about Paul. Mark advised Paul that he had told Dorian to continue with business as usual, since obviously this was very important for him. Paul waited for a few moments before speaking. He was confused as to why Mark had undermined his role within the team, and asked him for an explanation. Mark explained that Dorian appeared not to like Paul, and that he didn't want his team 'stressed'. Perhaps Paul was being too 'strict' on the project timetable. Paul reminded Mark that they had agreed the project plan and timetable, together with each participant's role, prior to the project being started. Although Mark conceded that Paul had actually followed the agreed plan of action, he seemed to feel that his team were 'uncomfortable' with the changes. Paul tried to explain that it was not unusual for people to feel uncomfortable at the beginning of a change programme, but felt that Mark had already made a decision.

The following day, Mark called Paul in and advised him that – in order to get the buy-in of Dorian – he had decided to put him in charge of the

> change project rather than Paul. Paul would – rather than lead the project – be more involved in undertaking actual project work.
>
> The remainder of the project, from Paul's perspective, was spent doing back-office work such as compiling statistics and spreadsheets. Dorian made any project work come second to business as usual. It was at this point that Paul decided to withdraw from the contract, and eventually the change project was put on hold.

I need to start by saying that the use of external consultants in change programmes, especially where there are sensitivities, complexities or short timescales involved, is a very sound strategy. If adequately trained in the area concerned, external consultants can greatly assist the company through the change process. What is important is how these consultants are utilised within the company.

The above scenarios reflect two of the most common problems experienced in making use of external consultants.

In the first scenario, the client has appointed someone who is a well-known speaker and obviously knows his stuff. Whilst one would expect this to be a very positive move for the company, in fact it ends up having the opposite effect. Harold makes a point of dealing specifically with the company executive team as opposed to working with the senior manager who appointed him, and obviously has no project management skills. He has successfully alienated the team almost immediately by disregarding any of their input and providing no actual leadership in the project.

So how could this situation have been avoided, and is what happened to Patrick Robertson typical of what happens when we bring in an 'elite' specialist for a project?

Well, the answer to the second question above is definitely 'No' – Patrick's experience – whilst not unique – is not typical just because the consultant is an elite specialist. I have dealt with a number of highly specialised consultants who have come into organisations and worked wonders. I have also seen a great many who could be Harold Davies' behavioural twin!

The way to ensure that you bring in the right specialist is to make sure that you have a proper assessment and interview process with them. Just because they are consultants does not make them exempt from the requirement for assessment. This assessment could take the form of a structured interview, being asked to develop a project plan from a case study, or to develop a formal presentation in response to a case study. It is also a good idea to try to get references from other companies who have used their services, although it is acknowledged that clients in certain industries will not authorise consultants to release their details and hence obtaining references may be challenging.

The second way to ensure that the external consultant is going to come in and undertake the project required of him or her is to involve some of the key members of the team in some of the pre-contractual meetings. I do not recommend that you invite them to attend the interviews (especially if they are going to be reporting to the consultant). Rather, have a specific day/time where you get members of the team together with the consultant once you are relatively confident that you are going to appoint them. Here you can introduce the consultant and give your team an opportunity to ask him or her about their background, skills and thoughts about the project, and, whilst making it clear that this person is pitching for the change project work, they therefore would be working for you to lead the change if they are successful.

This links into the second scenario, and a very important consideration in the appointment of an external consultant to run your change initiative. It is extremely important for the people in your team to know and understand that you have brought someone in to lead the change project, and as a result that he or she has your support and your delegated authority to undertake the programme.

I have already highlighted that as Asperger leaders we do sometimes feel challenged to delegate. Sometimes this takes the form of us delegating and then stepping too far back. We need to ensure that we retain overall responsibility by keeping an informal communication channel constantly open, but making sure there are regular update meetings, and by encouraging your team to come to you with any concerns. Most important, however, is the requirement that you reinforce that the external consultant is there to lead the project and therefore has your support.

Having said that, it is equally important for your team to understand *why* you have brought an external consultant in. If you have ambitious or enthusiastic people working for you, they may well feel undermined and very undervalued if you do not adequately explain your decision, since – in all likelihood – they would have been expecting to run with the project by themselves.

There is nothing wrong with bringing in an external consultant to control the change programme, but it is important to make sure you can clearly explain the reasons to your team. An external change consultant is generally brought in because they have a lot of experience in this area, and are good at project management. Another reason is that they can help provide support to the key people in your team and thereby free them up to get on with what they do best. A final reason is that they are from outside the organisation and therefore do not get caught up in some of the older 'office politics' all companies experience.

It is recommended that you have a team meeting – or at a minimum a meeting with the key people in your team – and advise them that you will be bringing in an external consultant to help them with the change programme, and explain why. You need to emphasise that you are doing this to assist them in order that the change occurs more easily and with less potential stress for the people in the team. Encourage them to make any comments on this decision, or ask any questions. If you do this, then by the time the consultant comes in to meet with the team, the difficult questions would already have been posed and the consultant should not be 'jumped on' from all sides!

There is another important point to consider. As you have seen in the second scenario, unless you are prepared to stand by your decision to appoint an external consultant and delegate authority to him or her, you will create frustration and inactivity in your team, and the project activity will decline, if not cease altogether. Very often I have seen situations where managers appoint consultants to come through and undertake significant change initiatives, only to buckle to staff pressures further down the line and end up either terminating the consultant's contract or putting them in a back-office or support role.

You, as manager, need to ensure that you take the concerns of your team seriously whilst making sure that you are not just falling foul of a type of undercurrent reaction to change. As you saw in Scenario 1, Patrick wasn't prepared to listen to the concerns of his Human Resources Manager and just dismissed them; whereas in Scenario 2, Mark accepted the word of his IT Manager over that of the consultant, without even discussing it with him – the complete opposite of Scenario 1. What should have occurred in both situations was a meeting with the manager, team-member and consultant, where the concerns could be discussed and any corrective actions taken. The situation with Mark was the most negative – the authority of the consultant was completely undermined by his actions, and there was – from that point forward – no way that he could positively contribute to the programme as a professional consultant.

I would like to end the chapter by summarising the key considerations when appointing a consultant:

- Always undertake some form of consultant assessment. If you are not sure how to do this, there are many organisations that can advise you – and it is often worthwhile speaking to your HR Director. Remember that cultural fit is as important as technical knowledge. If you find this an area of challenge for you, have a member of the human resources team undertake this part of the assessment for you.

- Make sure that the brief you provide to your consultant is specific and succinct. They should not be consulting to the executive team if they have been engaged by yourself, unless this has been agreed by you, since this represents trying to win additional business in the company.

- Get references from previous clients if you can.

- Speak to your team about the appointment of an external consultant, explaining the reason for their appointment.

- Make it clear that he or she is there to lead the project and will have your delegated authority.

- STICK TO YOUR COMMITMENT ABOVE.

- Give your team the opportunity to comment on your decision and ask questions before they meet the consultant.

- Make sure the team do meet with the consultant before you actually appoint him or her.

- If problems arise, discuss them together with the team-member and the consultant.

Chapter 23

Key Skill 11

Establishing a New Culture

By now the change programme is in the process of being rolled out or implemented, and a large number of the planned changes to operating systems, ways of working and business as usual are starting to be implemented.

If you have been successful in your change processes to date and have been able to apply the key skills identified so far, it is likely that your people have taken the change programme to heart and are fully engaged in the changes as they are taking place. This is a very important part of the change cycle, and not purely because your people are committed to the project. It is a time when people are very likely to be in the process of developing some new working practices to work best within the changing environment. As a result of having to deal with the situation of business-as-usual time commitments competing with change programme requirements, individuals will automatically begin to find ways to work more effectively and to develop 'leaner' processes. Change spurs creativity in working practices of necessity.

Now is the optimal time to start developing the new culture within your company or department. But what do we mean by this? Well, the best way to answer this is to define, first of all, what is meant by organisational culture.

What is an organisational culture?

Organisational culture can be defined in a number of ways, some of which we will expand upon briefly.

Geert Hofstede (1991) defines organisational culture as 'the collective programming of the mind which distinguishes members of one organisation from another' (p.5). Tichy (1982) defines what he calls corporate culture as the normative glue that holds an organisation together. Edgar Schein (2004) defines organisational culture as:

A pattern of shared basic assumptions that the groups learned as it solved its problems of external adaptation and internal integration, that has worked well enough to be considered valid and, therefore, to be taught to new members as the correct way to perceive, think and feel in relation to these problems. (p.17)

Seem like quite a few definitions? Well, as a matter of interest, Sackmann (1991) made the observation that there are 'almost as many definitions and understandings of culture as there are people writing about it' (p.2). However, the majority of them acknowledge the following constants:

- Organisational culture is historically determined.

- Organisational culture is socially constructed.

- Organisational culture is concerned with invisible assumptions and values.

- Organisational culture is difficult to change.

In short, organisational culture is the way of thinking, acting and feeling shared by the majority of people within a corporate body.

Notice that I have said that this is something that is shared by the *majority* of people in the organisation, not all. As you are no doubt aware, as people with Asperger syndrome it is highly likely that the culture of the organisation is not something that we are intuitively attuned to, and as a result we often have to 'adapt' our behaviours to ensure that these fit with how we interpret the culture to be. However, we are obviously not the only ones who are not necessarily aligned with the organisational culture. People new to the organisation and those going through a change in their mind-set or way of perceiving the company – all of these people may have a different feel for the organisational culture. However, in general, the organisational culture can be accurately described as the overall 'feel' within an organisation – its way of working, its way of business, its ethics – that the majority of people working there would be able to identify with and describe to someone from outside the company.

Understanding organisational sub-cultures

Despite our umbrella definition of organisational culture as set out above, it is important to understand that within an overall organisational culture there are many sub-cultures. Working in an organisation, I am sure that this is nothing new to you. People working within Operations talk about the 'feel' of the Finance Department, Human Resources complains about the 'flighty' mind-set in Marketing, and so on. Every area within the company that has a social identity of its own will have a slightly different culture, making the feel of the department comfortable (in most cases!) for the majority of people working there.

As mentioned, the organisational culture of a company generally consists of a number of sub-cultures, which is probably what we are going to be concentrating more on as we continue our discussions. A number of authors and academics have delved into the area of sub-cultures within organisations, and I hope to do them justice by summarising some of the key sub-cultural definitions here. My main aim is for you to be able to recognise and identify with them. Sub-cultures tend to develop into the following main types.

Elite versus Corporate culture

Louis (1985) elaborated on the development of the 'for-our-eyes-only' culture that develops at the top of an organisation. This is the Elite culture which emphasises that the leaders of the company are set apart from the rest of the company and that there is privileged information at this level of the organisation. Together with this is the element of the Corporate culture, the specially designed or tailored information and culture that the Elite allow to be passed down through the organisation. As this passes down through the entire company, it starts to create the actual organisational culture of the company, and hence you end up with the organisational culture tailored by the Elite culture.

Departmental culture

This is a sub-culture many of us can identify with through the descriptive name. It represents a horizontal slice through the organisation, such as the sales department or human resources department. A departmental sub-culture is related to the type of work being undertaken within that department. For example, you will find a very different culture within a marketing department to that of a finance department. The former is associated with energy, ideas and creativity, whilst the latter is associated with structure, set patterns and routine.

Divisional culture

Once again identified by Louis (1985), a divisional sub-culture is a vertical slice through the organisation, such as the risk management division of a financial institution, or the surveys division of a consultancy. What differentiates this from a departmental culture is that divisions tend to be micro- (and sometimes even mini-) organisations of their own. They have their own organisational structures, their own hierarchy and their own norms and practices.

Local culture

Guest, Peccei and Thomas (1994) reflect on a sub-culture determined by geographic region. We say that people situated in a different geographic area reflect a local culture. Differences in the culture could be caused by different environmental conditions, such as the country infrastructure, cultural context, management styles in that region, and so forth. Take another rather familiar example. Compare the local culture of the US division of a business with that of a European division. No matter which country we look at, there are going to be obvious differences.

Issue-related culture

This is a very interesting sub-culture. If you think about some areas of your business, you may find that they have a very specific focus to their operations and mind-set. For example, if you have a health and safety department or function, you will find that their focus is obviously on safety, compliance and process. But others could be areas of the business which have a specific focus on service, quality, time-management, and so on. Their focus is so specific that it creates an issue-related culture (Guest *et al.* 1994; Wilpert 1996).

Professional culture

The professional culture is based on having very specialised training or professional membership, for example brokers, accountants or academics. Due to people's training and professional standards, a certain code of conduct develops within this community of people, irrespective of where they work. I am sure you have heard comments along the lines of 'An actuary/accountant/ broker/consultant is the same, no matter who they work for.' Guest *et al.* (1994) note that this means this sub-culture can be inter-organisational. Depending on the nature of the company they work for, they can also form part of the overall culture of the organisation (as in the case of an actuary working within an actuarial firm) or of a departmental sub-culture (as in the example of a finance director within a marketing company).

Understanding organisational climate

Another subject you may have heard referred to in the context of considering organisational culture is that of organisational climate. This concept (which you may well have heard your human resources department referring to as the subject of a climate survey) is something which is closely related to, and yet different from, organisational culture.

Reiches and Schneider (1990) define climate as the common or shared perception of organisational policies, practices and procedures, both formal and informal. I would expand on that by adding that climate also includes people's perception of the company's current status (where are we as an organisation?) as well as how well the current culture is working.

If we relate organisational climate to organisational culture, it would be fair to say that organisational climate is a tangible manifestation of the underlying culture of the company. It is how people perceive and react to the current culture of the company. This is why climate surveys are undertaken to determine any underlying feelings or perceptions within the company that may influence behaviour and performance.

Whilst the organisational climate is obviously an important consideration in the day-to-day business environment, I am not going to focus on it to any great extent here for one fundamental reason: when companies go through change programmes, there will always be an element of dissatisfaction or uncertainty for some people, and as a result the climate survey will reflect this change in attitudes and perceptions. It is unlikely, therefore, to reflect accurate longer-term perceptions of your people. Whilst it certainly can act as an aid in determining the stability of the workplace, we are not going to focus on that application here.

Understanding your department or division's culture

In order to introduce a new culture within your division or department, it is important in the first instance to understand the current culture.

Part of the culture within your area will be determined by the way people work, both individually and as a team, which is one of the reasons that a change programme can have such a significant effect on morale. If the way people work is being forced to change, this will interfere with the culture that has been established and create a sense of dissatisfaction.

A key to overcoming this first hurdle has been created indirectly as a result of you preparing your team for change. In the same way that we tend to handle change better if we have had time to prepare for it, if people understand that a change is coming and can learn to embrace it, they will automatically start to let go of some of those rigid customs and practices that make up the current culture. Certainly, some things will be easier to let go of than others, but once the move has been made in the right direction it is easier to encourage additional changes towards a transitional culture.

Recognising the transitional culture

Once people have achieved that critical mind-set which allows them to let go of past culture and embrace change, they will start examining their work practices. As mentioned at the start of the chapter, change encourages creativity in working practices of necessity. Things cannot carry on as before. Sometimes there will be outside people coming in to assist in re-engineering the workings of the department, but on other occasions this will be down to people working in the department to sort it out for themselves. This results in a transitional culture developing in the workplace, where new practice and mind-sets are introduced and tried out.

At this time it is important for you, as leader, to act as both motivator and moderator. It is so important to encourage people to play an active role in developing new working practices. If you are involved in developing a new way of working, you are far more likely to take ownership and commit to the new system than if one is developed for you, no matter how much you agree with it.

At the same time, ideas about how to work in the change environment do need to be moderated by someone with an understanding of the bigger picture. Sometimes working practices which could potentially operate extremely well within one department could have a highly negative impact on the operation of another, or they could be of such a temporary nature that once the change programme was over, a whole new system of working would need to be designed. It is your responsibility as the leader of those people to ensure that they continue to be motivated, but have a reality check where and when necessary. And it needn't be said that in order for you to be able to do this, you need to be in touch with what people are doing, what they are feeling and how they are changing the current systems.

So let us summarise what we have covered so far. If all is going to plan with your change programme, the following things will be taking place:

- People will be engaged in the change process.

- People will have started to consider that there could be alternative ways of working.

- People will be starting to actively think about leaner and smarter ways of working.

- You will be acting as both moderator and motivator in respect of these activities.

But things don't end with developing new systems and mind-sets for the period of change as evidenced by a transitional culture. If you run your eyes back over the description of a culture, you will probably recognise that what has been happening here are the fundamentals of making your transitional culture into your permanent new culture.

Integrating your transitional culture into your permanent one

Your ultimate objective should be to ensure that the culture of revised working methods, positive attitudes and leaner or smarter working practices becomes established – not only as a transitional culture during the change process, but on an ongoing basis. Frequently, teams will develop fantastic ways of operating during a change programme that will save time and often money, but on completion of the change project itself the new practices slowly melt into the background, and old ways of operating revert to prominence, and as a result the floor drops out of the long-term change project.

A key part of the development of a new culture is reinforcement. Any coach or teacher will tell you that if you truly want to internalise something, the key is to practise, practise, practise. The same applies here. The more people are exposed to the new way of working and the ongoing nature of these new practices, the more they will 'stick'.

But there are other ways to ensure that these transitional practices become permanent ones. The first way to achieve this that is usually proposed is to include key features of the new methods in the performance appraisal system. Whilst there is nothing wrong with doing this, it should be kept in mind that this may be perceived as you trying to 'enforce' new behaviours rather than encouraging these ongoing behaviours.

I prefer to recommend that the integration of the new culture into the existing one be undertaken together with your people – after all, they are the ones who have been taking part in the changes to working practices and mind-set.

So how does one do this? Well, think about some of the ways that you learnt the established culture when you first joined the company (if you can remember back that far!). For most people this would initially be through their induction programme. Depending on how well this programme was done, you will find there were two key parts to that induction – the formal, practical, 'this is how we do things' part, and the 'this is us' part which covered the culture – be it formally or informally – of the company and/or department. This reflects a key part of learning a new culture – communicating what it is and how it is reflected.

Calling your team together and sharing with them that you want the current standards they have introduced to become part of the culture going forward is going to be a key element of ensuring this works. Let your people know you want their contributions to be ongoing and formalised. Ask them to assist in drawing up new operating manuals, or in the design of an appropriate induction toolkit. Ask them to volunteer for induction programmes for new staff in the future to ensure that they understand 'our way of working'.

Recognition is the strongest factor in establishing your new culture. Encourage the behaviours that are in line with your new culture; discourage behaviours that are not. But whatever you decide to do to ensure that the new culture is ingrained in your ongoing way of working, make sure that you also encourage a stage of renewal, as discussed in the following chapter.

Chapter 24

Key Skill 12

Applying the Fifth Transitional Stage of the Change Cycle

A sigh of relief often resounds through the organisation as a change programme is finally completed, although if you have been successful in your attempts to engage your people in the initiative, you may actually find an underlying sense of disappointment that the period of change is over, something you may not have expected.

In order to ensure the ongoing success of the new culture you have developed, as well as the focus you gained as a team in respect of encompassing change, it is extremely important that you regularly review the way you work and the environment in which you work as an ongoing activity.

If we look back at the psychological change cycle in Chapter 3, we can all identify with the fact that by the time we reach the end of the change programme and everything is established and operating smoothly, a phase of resolution or internalisation has been reached. As mentioned, this is a time when the new ways of working or thinking have become almost automatic, and the individual is comfortable operating in the new environment.

A great many leaders stop thinking about change at this time – after all, the programme is over and the change complete. But is that the best strategy?

In the majority of cases, a change programme takes place in order to improve some element of a business' performance or increase market opportunity. The time expended in undertaking the change would have been heavily weighted towards the front end of the process, where people needed to be moved from phases of denial and insecurity to those of acceptance, testing and reflection.

Thought leadership in the area of change tells us that change is not a one-off event. It is ongoing, only changing focus and intensity, but never truly ceasing. Certainly, as we continue to move from one change situation to another, it is better to have people who are proactively involved in the change process, rather than letting people settle into new established patterns before shaking the rug out from under them once again. Even a small change exercise can be traumatic if it is introduced after a large one that people have just 'recovered' from.

So how do we ensure that ongoing change can still occur without this being a problem for people? The answer to this lies in what I label the Fifth Transitional Stage of the Change Cycle – Renewal.

Transitional Stage 5: Renewal

In this final stage of transition, individuals take the time to review their new status in respect of changes that have recently taken place to determine whether any additional adjustments are worthwhile, or whether changes previously made are still relevant. It is during the time of renewal that people will ask questions such as 'That new operating system works well, but are there some better processes we can use to optimise the output?' or 'The new long-term incentive scheme seems to be well understood by the staff, but perhaps we should look at linking it more closely to the performance appraisal system?'

The purpose of the renewal stage is to ensure that the company or individual employees never become complacent in accepting where they currently are. In many cases, the renewal stage will end up being the precursor to another change cycle as people recognise what else can be done to ensure the company is always on the cutting edge. The main difference now is that the new change cycle will not be starting at Phase 1, since the people involved have already gone through their experience of numbness and denial as part of the original change initiative. Subsequent change initiatives will not result in the same degree of shock, numbness or denial experienced in any initial programme.

The five-stage transitional change cycle is illustrated in Figure 24.1.

In the majority of ongoing or further change initiatives, these generally originate at Phase 6 (contemplation) or Phase 7 (acknowledgement), and in some cases even as far along as Phase 8 (experimentation). The exception, of course, will be where an individual has not reached resolution, but has regressed instead. In this case, a further change programme will result in the initiation of a Stage 1 transitional response, which is likely to be more intense for the individual than the original one.

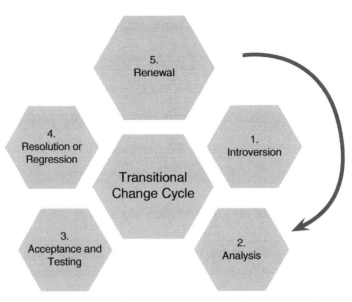

Figure 24.1 The five-stage transitional change cycle

How do I ensure we reach Stage 5?

It is important to realise that we cannot guarantee that people will automatically flow into Stage 5 of the transitional change cycle. Wherever possible, we need to ensure that this is the optimal route to follow, and there are a number of ways you can achieve this.

Encourage your team to identify potential areas of review

As mentioned earlier, people will automatically begin to consider the way they work when they have started to think in terms of the improvements a change programme has brought. The key for you as their leader is to encourage them to continue to identify those areas of review and not to feel that their efforts are either superfluous or 'being too niggly'. There are always people within the department or business who will be so pleased to see the end of a change programme that they would wish they could never look at another initiative in their lives. Deep down, most of us feel that way when the project first ends and we begin to wind down after a very busy period. But it is essential that people are made to feel that wanting to continue to improve things is not a character flaw, but an asset. You, of course, will act as the moderator on determining whether just too much change is being proposed or not. But in general, I recommend that you encourage them to keep a fresh mind on processes.

Action proposals, however small

A second recommendation is to action proposals made by your team, no matter how small or insignificant they may appear. Taking someone seriously is the best form of reinforcement, and if a member of your team comes forward with an idea for improvement which you subsequently act on and – potentially – implement, there is no better encouragement to keep it up!

Remember that when we talk about actioning a proposal, that does not mean that you are automatically going to be implementing it. What it means is that you are going to take it seriously and investigate it to see if it is a potentially viable piece of work for the future. So you will not just be saying to the team-member, 'Thanks Jim, that's nice. Put it down over there…' Instead, come up with a proc-ss for the review of ideas. Set a proposal format people should use to draft their ideas (without making this too constrained or extensive), and develop the actual mechanism for review. So, for example, you could say that proposals come to you in the first instance. These are then put to a team to review and potentially cost. If the proposal seems to be feasible, then a project team is identified, and so on.

The only thing that is critical for this process to be successful is for you to keep it dynamic. Make sure feedback is given to the team on how many people have come up with ideas, check with the team whether they think the review process is still relevant, and so on.

Reward successful proposals

This goes back to motivation. If someone spontaneously comes up with a proposal to review a process/activity that turns out to be successful and saves the company money/time, improves quality or such like, this needs to be recognised and rewarded. Once again, rewards can be intrinsic or extrinsic. They can be in terms of recognition in the company, or financial reward, or both! It needs to be relevant to the person and relevant to the proposal they have submitted.

Share successes with the business

I believe this is the most important element of ensuring that Transitional Stage 5 works within your team, and ultimately within your organisation. Share the success of your team with the business as a whole. Celebrate their successes and make their names known. After all, they are becoming the leading lights within the organisation by taking the time to look at how the company works and how to make it work better. They are your future change agents.

As the achievements of these key people are applauded in the business, this will start to influence other people who are outside your team. To be fair, it is likely to influence them in one of two ways. Some may be irritated or resentful of these people getting all the attention by suggesting even more change. Others will look at them and think, 'Why didn't I think of that?'

After all, Stage 5 of the transitional change cycle is not something you want to see occurring within just one area of the business. You want to see it flowing throughout the organisation as the company transforms to a learning organisation as opposed to a dinosaur.

My ultimate advice is to never take your team's creativity for granted.

Chapter 25

Summary and Application

Change is an integral part of becoming a leader in business. There is no such thing as leadership without it, no matter what people may imply or believe. Especially in today's economy and ever-changing marketplace, if we do not adapt we fall behind and ultimately lose out to the competition.

And so it is in our personal lives as well. Adaptation has always been a necessity for us – we constantly need to adjust to the neurotypical requirements around us, be it school, work or the social world. That just seems to be the way it is.

Whilst it may initially appear unfair that we are constantly having to change the way we work, the way we think and the way we encounter the world in favour of neurotypical society, in reality this has actually given us an advantage in the workplace that we need to recognise and make use of. Very few neurotypicals have had to work as hard as we have to adapt throughout life. To us it has become second nature. For most of them, the start of a change programme presents them with an entirely new situation that they find overwhelming.

I strongly believe that as leaders with Asperger syndrome we have significant benefits to offer to the organisations that recognise that talent. At the same time, it is essential that we ourselves recognise those talents as well, and have the confidence to be able to hold our heads up proudly and state, 'Yes, I do have Asperger syndrome.'

I hope that this book has provided some insights for you into some of the neurotypical journeys through change, and how a large change programme can affect your own behaviour. But more than anything I hope that this book has reassured you that there are many of us out there – Asperger leaders setting the example and acting as mentors in the organisations that we lead. Having a developmental 'disability' is not a handicap. In some respects it is a significant asset. I hope that you will make use of the further books in the series as part of your ongoing career development as you progress to be an even more successful leader in your organisation and in your country.

PART 4

Practical Tools for Asperger Leaders Leading Change

YOUR PSYCHOLOGICAL REACTION TO CHANGE VERSUS NEUROTYPICAL REACTIONS

In Chapter 3 we discussed the transitional stages and the psychological change cycle. This exercise gives you the opportunity to reflect on your own reaction within the psychological change cycle, as well as considering how best to assist any of your employees within the various stages.

Bring to mind a significant change event in your personal experience that affected you and at least one other person. This does not have to be work-related, but needs to be significant enough to have had an influence on you personally. Keeping the event in mind, work through Exercise Table 1.1 in respect of the different phases of the psychological change cycle, considering whether or not you are able personally to identify with each stage, and giving some indication of how you reacted in each stage, and how the other person/people appeared to act. If you cannot think of a change event where other people were involved, complete this exercise for yourself only.

Think about some of the main ways in which your own handling of change differed from the neurotypical handling of change. In what ways did you appear to have the same or similar reaction? In what ways were your reactions very different to those of neurotypicals? Are there any ways that you can think of to share your coping mechanisms (where they have been beneficial to you) with people who could be struggling with change?

Exercise Table 1.1

Psychological change cycle	In what ways did your behaviour reflect this phase?	In what ways did other people's behaviour reflect this phase?
Shock/numbness		
Denial		
Defensive blaming		
Panic/dread		
Depression/insecurity		
Contemplation		
Acknowledgement		

cont.

Psychological change cycle	In what ways did your behaviour reflect this phase?	In what ways did other people's behaviour reflect this phase?
Experimentation		
Discovery/learning		
Reflection		
Optimism or uncertainty		
Satisfaction or dissatisfaction		
Integration or withdrawal		

TOOLKIT EXERCISE 2

HANDLING DELEGATION

In Chapter 11 we discussed the problems leaders with Asperger syndrome sometimes experience when it comes to delegation during a period of change. This exercise is aimed at helping you identify if you are starting to 'hug to the chest' as a result of a disruption to your normal working routine.

Part 1

Consider a period of time approximately six months ago. The time period can be less than this, provided that it is before any change activity started. Think about some key tasks that you have delegated to members of your team. If possible, access your calendar or any records where you note information in respect of delegated items. Find at least ten key tasks that you would regularly delegate, ensuring that they are at various levels of accountability. I need you to consider what type of task this represented (e.g. administrative, research based, confidential, team-based, project-based, executive-level), what level of accountability you delegated (full, partial, limited), and the general reporting/monitoring you used at that time. Record the information in Exercise Table 2.1.

For example, one of your tasks could be delegation of responsibility for determining a new customer relationship management (CRM) system for marketing. This could have been delegated with full control of the project, and it could have been agreed that the manager concerned provide you with a full proposal within two weeks. Alternatively, it could have been delegated with set parameters for what type of system to research, with a requirement for the manager to meet with you weekly to feed back results to date, and ultimately for the manager to advise about findings so that you could write up a report. These are examples of two very different levels of delegation. In this exercise, you should try to give more focus on more executive, team-based and confidential delegation rather than routine administrative delegation.

Exercise Table 2.1

Task or accountability delegated: historic	Type of task	Level of accountability	Monitoring/ reporting agreed	How often is this type of task delegated?

Part 2

In the second part of the exercise, think again of some of the tasks that you have been delegating. If possible, try to use the same sorts of tasks you have used in the first part of the exercise. Complete Exercise Table 2.2 in respect of these activities.

Exercise Table 2.2

Task or accountability delegated: current	Type of task	Level of accountability	Monitoring/ reporting agreed	How often is this type of task delegated?

Part 3

Answer the questions in Exercise Table 2.3 in respect of your delegation as a whole.

Exercise Table 2.3

	Previously	**Currently**
In general, how many tasks did/do you delegate per month?		
How many people did/ do you delegate to?		
How many confidential or high-priority tasks did/ do you generally delegate per month?		
How frequently did/ do you meet with subordinates in respect of delegated tasks?		
How many administrative tasks did/do you delegate per month on average?		

Are there any tasks you can identify as being 'instructions' as opposed to delegation?		
What feedback did/ do you receive from subordinates regarding delegation?		
Did/do you agree the plan of action with subordinates or do you allow them to decide that themselves?		
Approximately what percentage of your time was/is spent on routine tasks?		

Having completed the exercises, you should be able to see if your behaviour in respect of delegation has changed significantly since the start of your change programme. Keep in mind that you are not only looking for indications that you are starting to 'hug to the chest' rather than delegate; you are also looking for instances where you are potentially 'dumping' rather than delegating, or 'instructing' rather than delegating.

After completing the above activity, spend a few minutes considering where you can take action, additional areas where you need to delegate, and so forth, and note them below.

TOOLKIT EXERCISE 3
HANDLING YOUR REACTION TO CHANGE

In Chapter 13 we discussed the ways that change can affect you personally, and how periods of intense change work can potentially interfere with your regular coping strategies. Whilst it is possible that your current coping strategies will be more than effective for the period of change, it is worthwhile taking the time to be aware of when the pressures of change are beginning to affect your behaviour. In this exercise, you are encouraged to think about some of the behaviours you needed to develop coping strategies across different phases of your life.

Part 1: Your individual behaviours

Exercise Tables 3.1 to 3.3 show some of the more common issues experienced by those of us with Asperger syndrome, and allow you to indicate the degree to which these were representative of your behaviour in that phase of your life.

High school

Take some time to think about the behaviours/challenges you experienced in high school. Indicate in the appropriate boxes in Exercise Table 3.1 those areas where you experienced challenges and the appropriate level of challenge.

Exercise Table 3.1

My key behavioural indicators at high school	Does not apply	Mild or irregular	Quite often	Regularly	Almost all the time	Key problem area
Aggression/overly assertive						
Isolating oneself						
Anxiety						
Depression						
Tantrums/outbursts						
Inability or difficulty making friends						
Problems with teamwork						
Problems with conversations (inappropriate comments, speaking too fast/slow, interrupting others, going off topic)						
Rituals or compulsive behaviours						
Specialist interest being focal						
Difficulties understanding other people's thoughts or reactions (mindblindness)						
Sensory hypersensitivities						
Poor coordination and/or balance						
Stimming behaviour						
Problems interpreting instructions (taking things too literally)						
Very blunt/matter of fact with opinions						

Problems with personal body language (lack of or inappropriate facial expressions, gestures or actions, inappropriate stimming)					
Problems interpreting body language in others					
Problems with eye contact					
Problems with proximity/personal space					
Hypervigilance					
Inability to focus on a task due to distractions					
Getting too caught up in the details of an assignment without being able to see the overview (e.g. writing a detailed essay but not being able to summarise it appropriately)					
Perfectionism (struggling to leave tasks until they are perfect)					
Difficulty with verbal directions or instructions					
Dependent on instructions; not being proactive					
Insistence of doing things 'your way' and no other					
Problems multitasking					
Sensory overload					
Shutdown or deliberate isolation					
Others (detail)					

Early work experiences

Take some time to think about the behaviours/challenges you experienced during your early working experience. Indicate in the appropriate boxes in Exercise Table 3.2 those areas where you experienced challenges and the appropriate level of challenge.

Exercise Table 3.2

My key behavioural indicators in my early career	Does not apply	Mild or irregular	Quite often	Regularly	Almost all the time	Key problem area
Aggression/overly assertive						
Isolating oneself						
Anxiety						
Depression						
Tantrums/outbursts						
Inability or difficulty making friends						
Problems with teamwork						
Problems with conversations (inappropriate comments, speaking too fast/slow, interrupting others, going off topic)						
Rituals or compulsive behaviours						
Specialist interest being focal						
Difficulties understanding other people's thoughts or reactions (mindblindness)						
Sensory hypersensitivities						
Poor coordination and/or balance						
Stimming behaviour						
Problems interpreting instructions (taking things too literally)						
Very blunt/matter of fact with opinions						

Problems with personal body language (lack of or inappropriate facial expressions, gestures or actions, inappropriate stimming)					
Problems interpreting body language in others					
Problems with eye contact					
Problems with proximity/personal space					
Hypervigilance					
Inability to focus on a task due to distractions					
Getting too caught up in the details of an assignment without being able to see the overview (e.g. writing a detailed essay but not being able to summarise it appropriately)					
Perfectionism (struggling to leave tasks until they are perfect)					
Difficulty with verbal directions or instructions					
Dependent on instructions; not being proactive					
Insistence of doing things 'your way' and no other					
Problems multitasking					
Problems delegating					
Sensory overload					
Shutdown or deliberate isolation					
Others (detail)					

Current work experiences

Take some time to think about the behaviours/challenges you currently experience at your present level of seniority in your career. Indicate in the appropriate boxes in Exercise Table 3.3 those areas where you currently experience challenges and the appropriate level of challenge.

Exercise Table 3.3

My current key behavioural indicators	Does not apply	Mild or irregular	Quite often	Regularly	Almost all the time	Key problem area
Aggression/overly assertive						
Isolating oneself						
Anxiety						
Depression						
Tantrums/outbursts						
Inability or difficulty making friends						
Problems with teamwork						
Problems with conversations (inappropriate comments, speaking too fast/slow, interrupting others, going off topic)						
Rituals or compulsive behaviours						
Specialist interest being focal						
Difficulties understanding other people's thoughts or reactions (mindblindness)						
Sensory hypersensitivities						
Poor coordination and/or balance						
Stimming behaviour						
Problems interpreting instructions (taking things too literally)						
Very blunt/matter of fact with opinions						

Problems with personal body language (lack of or inappropriate facial expressions, gestures or actions, inappropriate stimming)						
Problems interpreting body language in others						
Problems with eye contact						
Problems with proximity/personal space						
Hypervigilance						
Inability to focus on a task due to distractions						
Getting too caught up in the details of an assignment without being able to see the overview (e.g. writing a detailed essay but not being able to summarise it appropriately)						
Perfectionism (struggling to leave tasks until they are perfect)						
Difficulty with verbal directions or instructions						
Dependent on instructions; not being proactive						
Insistence of doing things 'your way' and no other						
Problems multitasking						
Problems delegating						
Sensory overload						
Shutdown or deliberate isolation						
Others (detail)						

Part 2: Understanding your individual behaviours

Have a look at Exercise Tables 3.1 to 3.3 and think about how your behaviours have changed over the periods indicated. What actions or coping strategies have you developed to assist you in managing difficult situations? Were there any particular situations/activities you found it better to avoid/change to bring your inconsistent behaviours under control?

_____

_____

_____

_____

_____

Part 3: Previous reactions to change

Think about some changes you may have experienced during the three phases indicated above. In each case, consider how you initially reacted to the change, how you managed going forward and any changes to your key behavioural indicators. Ask yourself the following questions:

1. At what point did the change become uncomfortable for me?

2. Can I identify what part of the change began to result in a change in my behaviour?

3. Which behaviours that I had previously altered or reduced did I revert to as a result of my reaction to the change?

4. How did I resolve the issue at the time?

5. Is there anything that I would have done differently had I understood that my key behavioural indicators were changing?

_____

_____

_____

_____

_____

_____

_____

_____

_____

_____

Part 4: Coping strategies for key behavioural indicators

Having thought about your key behavioural indicators and how you
have managed them over time, spend some time thinking of coping
strategies that would be appropriate for you to utilise should your
behaviour regress in any particular area. In addition, think about how
you would recognise if your behaviours were regressing. This will help
you to be more aware if this actually starts happening in reaction to
a change programme, and will allow you more time to adjust your
coping strategies. Record the information in Exercise Table 3.4.

Exercise Table 3.4

	How will changes in this area manifest?	Proposed practical coping strategies
Aggression/overly assertive		
Isolating oneself		
Anxiety		
Depression		
Tantrums/outbursts		
Inability or difficulty making friends		
Problems with teamwork		

Problems with conversations (inappropriate comments, speaking too fast/slow, interrupting others, going off topic)						
Rituals or compulsive behaviours						
Specialist interest being focal						
Difficulties understanding other people's thoughts or reactions (mindblindness)						
Sensory hypersensitivities						
Poor coordination and/or balance						
Stimming behaviour						
Problems interpreting instructions (taking things too literally)						

	How will changes in this area manifest?	Proposed practical coping strategies
Very blunt/matter of fact with opinions		
Problems with personal body language (lack of or inappropriate facial expressions, gestures or actions, inappropriate stimming)		
Problems interpreting body language in others		
Problems with eye contact		
Problems with proximity/personal space		
Hypervigilance		
Inability to focus on a task due to distractions		

Getting too caught up in the details of an assignment without being able to see the overview (e.g. writing a detailed essay but not being able to summarise it appropriately)	
Perfectionism (struggling to leave tasks until they are perfect)	
Difficulty with verbal directions or instructions	
Dependent on instructions; not being proactive	
Insistence of doing things 'your way' and no other	
Problems multitasking	
Problems delegating	

cont.

	How will changes in this area manifest?	Proposed practical coping strategies
Sensory overload		
Shutdown or deliberate isolation		
Others (detail)		

TOOLKIT EXERCISE 4

HANDLING CHALLENGES IN MEETINGS

In Chapter 19 we discussed the importance of identifying and dealing with undercurrents within the company as a whole. Very often, as a consequence of where people are in their own experience of the change cycle, individuals may exhibit behaviours which are disruptive or dysfunctional. This happens more often than not in a group environment where individuals can influence others and make sure they are aware of what they may perceive as non-conformational opinions. In order to ensure the effectiveness of meetings and workshops, it is important for everyone in the meeting to play a part in keeping the meeting on track. Ultimately, however, it is the leader's responsibility to ensure that the meetings are redirected and that any negative behaviour is curtailed in an assertive but positive way. By doing this, the leader will be ensuring that the meeting achieves its objectives, and also that the confidence of other participants within the meeting is maintained.

As a leader with Asperger syndrome, it is essential that we are confident in handling potential conflicts in such things as meetings and workshops relating to the change programme. Whilst neurotypicals may appear to know intuitively how to recognise and address inappropriate behaviour, this can be more challenging for us.

This exercise provides you with an opportunity to rehearse some of the techniques that we discussed in Chapter 19, as well as potentially covering some additional areas covered in Chapter 20. I suggest that you complete Part 1 of the exercise now, and return to Parts 2–4 at the indicated place in Chapter 19.

The purpose of the following exercise is two-fold. In the first instance, you will be given an opportunity to consider a number of situations where some dysfunctional behaviour is taking place in a group setting, and to determine how you would handle these as leader. The second part of the exercise will provide you with a number of potential responses to the same situations, which you will be required to rank in order of which is the most appropriate response to which is the least appropriate response. In the third and fourth parts, you will be able to assess how your initial responses compared to the standard responses provided in the second part.

Part 1: Your insights

A number of scenarios are presented where some dysfunctional behaviour is being displayed. Take some time to read each scenario and consider how you would react to this situation. Then put down what you would say to the person concerned and any additional actions you may take. It is important that you write this down as you believe you would say it. For example, rather than saying 'I would tell him not to discuss that matter during the workshop' you would rather say 'Matthew, please don't talk about that now.' You shouldn't spend more than five minutes on each scenario.

Scenario 1: Change programme meeting

At the initiation of a change management programme in the organisation, a number of focus groups are being held across the organisation where key members of the programme team attend workshops with employees followed by focus group question sessions. You have noticed that one of the team-members, Ben, does not appear to be participating in the discussions and frequently looks down to read emails on his phone. As you continue answering some questions directed to the team by an employee, you notice that Ben is now talking with another member of the team about something not related to the change programme. How would you handle this situation?

_____

_____

_____

_____

_____

Scenario 2: Committee meeting

A committee meeting has been scheduled to discuss the shortage of project managers across the human resources department. As Amy Henderson, Head of Human Resources, begins to make her presentation covering the need for interim project managers in the department, Jeremy Miles (Finance Officer) interrupts with the comment, 'I don't see any point in this meeting since there simply aren't any additional funds for this programme if we need extra staff.' As chairman of the meeting, how would you respond?

_____

_____

_____

_____

_____

Scenario 3: Committee meeting challenges at another level

As the committee progresses, you notice that Amy Henderson keeps referring to an error in last month's financial reports for the programme generated by Jeremy's team. The error was a minor one which was corrected, and the matter is irrelevant to the present discussion. As chairman of the meeting, how would you respond?

_____

_____

_____

_____

_____

Scenario 4: A situation we can identify with

You have been advised by one of your project managers that there seems to be a situation arising in one of the project teams, and you have been asked to attend one of their meetings to assist the group in making a final decision. At the meeting, it becomes apparent that every time Matthew Barker, Head of Operations, has been asked for his opinion, he has stated that he needs more information and further study of the situation before he can comment. This appears to be his response on every area of the project. What would you say to Matthew to move the meeting on?

_____

_____

_____

_____

_____

Scenario 5: Programme review meeting

You are chairing a quarterly review meeting of a key programme for the business. Ken Arkle, Head of Procurement, arrived quite late and now announces that he needs to leave for another meeting (in respect of the procurement of some new computer equipment). What would you say to Ken?

_____

_____

_____

_____

_____

I suggest you return to your reading in Chapter 19 at this point. You will be directed back to Parts 2–4 of the exercise at the appropriate point in your reading.

Part 2: Recognising best options

Here the scenarios from Part 1 are revisited. This time, however, you are presented with some possible answers to the questions. You need to rank these suggestions from 1 to 3, with 1 being the most appropriate response and 3 being the least appropriate response. Again, you should spend no more than five minutes on each scenario.

Scenario 1: Change programme meeting

At the initiation of a change management programme in the organisation, a number of focus groups are being held across the organisation where key members of the programme team attend workshops with employees followed by focus group question sessions. You have noticed that one of the team-members, Ben, does not appear to be participating in the discussions and frequently looks down to read emails on his phone. As you continue answering some questions directed to the team by an employee, you notice that Ben is now talking with another member of the team about something not related to the change programme. Possible responses are:

RANK	RESPONSE
———	1. You pause in mid-sentence in response to an employee's question and look at Ben without comment, or perhaps adding 'Ben, perhaps all the employees would like to hear what you have to say?'
———	2. 'Ben, would you please direct your attention to the matter being discussed?'
———	3. 'Perhaps Ben would be the best member of the team to answer your question. Ben?'

Scenario 2: Committee meeting

A committee meeting has been scheduled to discuss the shortage of project managers across the human resources department. As Amy Henderson, Head of Human Resources, begins to make her presentation covering the need for interim project managers in the department, Jeremy Miles (Finance Officer) interrupts with the comment, 'I don't see any point in this meeting since there simply aren't any additional funds for this programme if we need extra staff.' Possible responses are:

RANK	RESPONSE
———	1. 'If you really think that, Jeremy, why did you even come to the meeting?'
———	2. 'How do the rest of you feel about proceeding with the meeting, given Jeremy's reservations?'
———	3. 'That's precisely why you were invited to this meeting, Jeremy, because only you can identify potential sources of funding if the group decides the staffing need must be met.'

Scenario 3: Committee meeting challenges at another level

As the committee progresses, you notice that Amy Henderson keeps referring to an error in last month's financial reports for the programme generated by Jeremy's team. The error was a minor one which was corrected, and the matter is irrelevant to the present discussion.

RANK	RESPONSE
———	1. 'As you are aware, Amy, that error was corrected very promptly, and I'm sure you will agree that Jeremy is the best person to advise on the financial issues we face today.'
———	2. 'Amy, can you explain to us why you feel that point is relevant to this meeting?'
———	3. 'Amy, I know Jeremy challenged you just now, but let's keep this meeting professional, shall we?'

Scenario 4: A situation we can identify with

You have been advised by one of your project managers that there seems to be a situation arising in one of the project teams, and you have been asked to attend one of their meetings to assist the group in making a final decision. At the meeting, it becomes apparent that every time Matthew Barker, Head of Operations, has been asked for his opinion, he has stated that he needs more information and further study of the situation before he can comment. This appears to be his response on every area of the project. Suggested responses are:

RANK	RESPONSE
———	1. 'Matthew, you've analysed this project to death. It's time to move on.'
———	2. 'Where, specifically, do you think we need more information, Matthew?'
———	3. 'Whilst I appreciate your diligence in wanting to analyse the project further – and we certainly appreciate your insights here believe that the time has now come to make a decision on the basis of the information we do have.'

Scenario 5: Programme review meeting

You are chairing a quarterly review meeting of a key programme for the business. Ken Arkle, Head of Procurement, arrived quite late and now announces that he needs to leave for another meeting (in respect of the procurement of some new computer equipment). Suggested responses are:

RANK	RESPONSE
————	1. 'Since you've only just got here, Ken, don't you think you should stay a while longer?'
————	2. 'For goodness sake, Ken, why on earth are you booking overlapping meetings?'
————	3. 'Alright, Ken, but perhaps we can discuss this later to ensure that this sort of issue doesn't arise again?'

Part 3: Answers to Part 2

Have a look at the proposed ranking for the scenarios presented in Part 2 of the exercise, and make a note of how your rankings compare. Score your answer as follows: Correct ranking scores 1, incorrect ranking scores 0.

Scenario 1: Change programme meeting

At the initiation of a change management programme in the organisation, a number of focus groups are being held across the organisation where key members of the programme team attend workshops with employees followed by focus group question sessions. You have noticed that one of the team-members, Ben, does not appear to be participating in the discussions and frequently looks down to read emails on his phone. As you continue answering some questions directed to the team by an employee, you notice that Ben is now talking with another member of the team about something not related to the change programme.

In change management terms, what Ben is doing is known as side-tracking. This is when someone can try to take the focus of the meeting or group off track by either introducing irrelevant issues or by causing a disruption. This does not mean that the person is necessarily being intentionally disruptive. It could be that they just lack the mental discipline to stay focused. Either way, the treatment should be the same.

RESPONSE	CORRECT RANK	YOUR RANK	YOUR SCORE
You pause mid-sentence in response to an employee's question and look at Ben without comment, or perhaps add, 'Ben, perhaps all the employees would like to hear what you have to say?' *OBSERVATION: If you were in a closed meeting and Ben was ignoring presentations from either yourself or others in the meeting, this would actually be the best response, since it is an effective use of silence. However, in an open meeting, this would make it very obvious to the employees that there is an issue with Ben, and this would be inappropriate – both from the perspective of the employees seeing you challenge Ben and your raising it to their attention.*	2		
'Ben, would you please direct your attention to the matter being discussed?' *OBSERVATION: This response not only disciplines Ben in front of employees (some of whom could report to him) but could affect the openness of the workgroup, since employees may feel uncomfortable making any comments in case they receive similar feedback if it is not considered appropriate.*	3		
'Perhaps Ben would be the best member of the team to answer your question. Ben?' *OBSERVATION: This response is the most effective in an employee-facing workshop, since it will bring Ben to the centre of attention where he needs to be focused to respond. It should also act as a reminder to Ben that he needs to stay focused to ensure he can answer further questions without prompting.*	1		

Scenario 2: Committee meeting

A committee meeting has been scheduled to discuss the shortage of project managers across the human resources department. As Amy Henderson, Head of Human Resources, begins to make her presentation covering the need for interim project managers in the department, Jeremy Miles (Finance Officer) interrupts with the comment, 'I don't see any point in this meeting since there simply aren't any additional funds for this programme if we need extra staff.'

In change management terms, this represents a situation of rejection and rebellion against the change. It is a type of dysfunctional behaviour that is relatively common, especially in the earlier stages of a change programme. It is important not to let the individual concerned sabotage the programme by introducing doubts or delays.

RESPONSE	CORRECT RANK	YOUR RANK	YOUR SCORE
'If you really think that, Jeremy, why did you come to the meeting?' *OBSERVATION: This is a negative confrontation. This will encourage a negative – possibly angry – response and the person attempting to disrupt the meeting will actually have succeeded in what he was trying to achieve.*	3		
'How do the rest of you feel about proceeding with the meeting, given Jeremy's reservations?' *OBSERVATION: By responding this way, you are providing a potential 'exit route' for anyone finding the change programme challenging, and acknowledging that there could be grounds to cancel the change programme. If the leadership of the company has committed to the change programme, you should not be encouraging the committee to challenge this based on the input of one person. Ultimately, should that situation arise, you would be the one to identify the need and present it to the Board.*	2		

'That's precisely why you were invited to this meeting, Jeremy, because only you can identify potential sources of funding if the group decides the staffing need must be met.'	
OBSERVATION: This is a good response for a number of reasons. First, it keeps Jeremy involved in the discussion and therefore does not create any divisions. It could also reaffirm to Jeremy his role in the group as a valuable adviser rather than as the ultimate decision maker. It also allows the other committee members to be aware of Jeremy's concerns, and to take these into consideration when making a decision.	1

Scenario 3: Committee meeting challenges at another level

As the committee progresses, you notice that Amy Henderson keeps referring to an error in last month's financial reports for the programme generated by Jeremy's team. The error was a minor one which was corrected, and the matter is irrelevant to the present discussion.

In change management terms, this is what is known as countering. It is apparent that Amy has felt challenged by Jeremy and is retaliating by attacking his team's competency and credibility. The problem is caused by difficulties between individuals who may be feeling challenged or stressed, and may not be caused by the actual change process, but purely exacerbated by it. In any event, for the meeting to be productive, it is essential that this behaviour is addressed early.

RESPONSE	CORRECT RANK	YOUR RANK	YOUR SCORE
'As you are aware, Amy, that error was corrected very promptly, and I'm sure you will agree that Jeremy is the best person to advise on the financial issues we face today.' *OBSERVATION: This response redirects Amy to the focus of the meeting, whilst acknowledging indirectly that Jeremy may be feeling 'under attack'. It should reassure Jeremy that he does not need to defend himself or his team. In addition, Amy also has the opportunity to neutralise the situation by agreeing with you and thereby acknowledging her support of Jeremy's role.*	1		
'Amy, can you explain to us why you feel that point is relevant to this meeting?' *OBSERVATION: This will give Amy the opportunity either to explain why she is raising the issue or to step back, and will also make it apparent that you recognised her countering attempt and that this sort of behaviour will be challenged.*	2		
'Amy, I know Jeremy challenged you just now, but let's keep this meeting professional, shall we?' *OBSERVATION: This is a very negative response. It both undermines Amy in the meeting and openly ridicules how she is feeling about Jeremy's challenge. This will, in all likelihood, cause Amy to withdraw from contributing further to the meeting, and is likely to fuel ongoing antagonism between Jeremy and Amy.*	3		

Scenario 4: A situation we can identify with

You have been advised by one of your project managers that there seems to be a situation arising in one of the project teams, and you have been asked to attend one of their meetings to assist the group in making a final decision. At the meeting, it becomes apparent that every time Matthew Barker, Head of Operations, has been asked for his opinion, he has stated that he needs more information and further study of the situation before he can comment. This appears to be his response on every area of the project.

In change management terms, what is happening here is often termed 'paralysis by analysis'. We need to be careful to distinguish between this and the way we frequently tend to want a lot of detailed information ourselves. Whilst we may want a lot of information and, as Asperger leaders, tend to analyse it in significant detail, we would actually do it and return to the meeting with the results of the data analysis rather than saying it needs to be done and not doing it. In this situation, the person concerned is quite possibly in denial, and is trying to avoid making decisions or acknowledging that the change needs to occur.

RESPONSE	CORRECT RANK	YOUR RANK	YOUR SCORE
'Matthew, you've analysed this project to death. It's time to move on.' OBSERVATION: This response is both undermining and derogatory. It is likely to have the effect of causing Matthew to become silent in the meeting whilst becoming antagonistic towards the change programme itself.	3		
'Where, specifically, do you think we need more information, Matthew?' OBSERVATION: Whilst this is a more positive response, it does potentially encourage delays. It also causes Matthew to feel undervalued if he then explains where he feels information is needed but this is not acted on.	2		
'Whilst I appreciate your diligence in wanting to analyse the project further – and we certainly appreciate your insights here – I believe that the time has now come to make a decision on the basis of the information we do have.' OBSERVATION: This response acknowledges Matthew's expertise and concerns as well as focusing the group on the process of decision making. It emphasises the completion of the task without undermining Matthew's contribution.	1		

Scenario 5: Programme review meeting

You are chairing a quarterly review meeting of a key programme for the business. Ken Arkle, Head of Procurement, arrived quite late and now announces that he needs to leave for another meeting (in respect of the procurement of some new computer equipment).

There are number of potential reasons for this behaviour. If the behaviour is habitual, of course, this is a time-management issue for the individual concerned. However, if it is out of character, there could be three main reasons for this. First, Ken could be trying to impress on the group how valuable he is outside the programme itself. Second, he could be finding the increased responsibilities involved with the change programme a challenge. Third – and potentially most negative – Ken could be passively resisting the change by showing how unimportant this is to the company business as usual.

RESPONSE	CORRECT RANK	YOUR RANK	YOUR SCORE
'Since you've only just got here, Ken, don't you think you should stay a while longer?' OBSERVATION: *This response emphasises the fact that Ken arrived late, and the fact that you are seemingly accepting that diminishes the importance of the programme review meeting for the others present. Also, Ken could take this as a sarcastic comment (although it is unlikely that you would intend it that way, since we tend not to do sarcasm all that well), which could raise animosity.*	2		
'For goodness sake, Ken, why on earth are you booking overlapping meetings?' OBSERVATION: *This is an emotional response rather than a positive one, and encourages Ken to go into detail about just how busy he is. This ultimately would service his underlying agenda rather than that of the meeting.*	3		

'Alright, Ken, but perhaps we can discuss this later to ensure that this sort of issue doesn't arise again?'		
OBSERVATION: This response acknowledges Ken needs to leave the meeting whilst making it clear that this is unacceptable behaviour. It will also reassure other members of the meeting who may be feeling frustrated with Ken that the situation is being addressed.	1	

Part 4: Analysis

Compare the original answers you supplied in Part 1 of the exercise with the choices you made in Part 2 and ultimately the answers in Part 3. Think about how your responses reflect how you could have influenced the change programme. Perhaps ask yourself the following questions:

1. Which of my responses would have created animosity between others?

2. Which of my answers indicate that I am not recognising others' contributions?

3. Which type of situation did I do best in?

4. Which type of situation did I do worst in?

RECOGNISING THE DIFFERENT TYPES OF CHANGE AGENTS

In Chapter 21 we discussed the importance of identifying and developing change agents within your organisation to help drive the progression and ultimate success of your change programme. As was noted in that chapter, however, there are different types of change agents with whom you will come into contact, and it is important that you are able to identify the differences between them.

Chapter 21 detailed the differences between Messengers and Advocates. The following exercise provides you with the opportunity to identify these from some practical examples, as well as to think about some additional characteristics.

Consider the following scenario and the approaches made to you as the leader of a change programme by members of your team, and then answer the questions that follow:

> Century Publishing is in the process of merging its operations with a previously separate subsidiary, Century Printing. As a result of the merger, you have been appointed as the sponsor for the change programme, and are leading the organisation through its operational, branding and marketing integration.
>
> A few weeks into the change programme you are approached separately by two individuals from different areas of the business. Jake, from the newly formed Digital Print marketing team, approaches you one morning as you are preparing for your day.
>
> *Jake*: Hi, John. How are you?
>
> *You*: Hello, Jake. I am well, thank you.
>
> *Jake*: I know you're busy, but do you mind if I come in and close the door? There's something I need to discuss with you.
>
> *You*: Of course. How can I help you?
>
> *Jake*: Well, I just thought I should let you know that there is a bit of concern amongst the team about the possibility of redundancies within the company. I know that you said that there wouldn't be any, but people are still very worried about it. I have told them I didn't think they needed to worry – if there was any possibility of that you would have told us. But I think that you need to be aware of how unsettled people are feeling right now.

About an hour after Jake has spoken to you, Erica, the head receptionist, rings you and asks to speak with you. You invite her to your office and she comes in and stands at the door. You invite her to take a seat. She smiles, then quickly sits down.

You: Now, Erica, what did you want to discuss with me?

Erica smiles, gives a sort of chuckle, and clears her throat.

Erica: Well Mr Kingsley, my receptionists, Patricia and Marcy, told me they needed to know how their jobs will be affected by the change as far as overtime rates go.

Erica stops speaking and looks down at her hands, then out to the window. You wait for her to continue, but when she doesn't you speak.

You: Alright.

Erica glances at you, then back down at her hands.

Erica: I told them I would bring it up with you.

You: I'm glad you did, Erica. Shall we talk about it now?

Erica looks up quickly, suddenly animated and quickly getting to her feet.

Erica: Oh no, no. I was just letting you know what they were concerned about. I'm sure they would be happy to hear from you directly.

Later in the day, you are approached in the corridor by Gina, a member of the human resources team, whilst you are speaking with another member of the leadership team.

Gina: John, I need to talk to you.

You: Of course. Are you happy to speak here or would you prefer to come to my office?

Gina: Your office, I think.

Gina nods and precedes you into your office, where she turns and waits for you to close the door.

Gina: A number of people have been complaining about the lack of career opportunities this merger will result in. We feel that this means that our rights to career development have been interfered with. This is something you need to think about, because it is a serious issue and the people concerned about this are the sort of people you do not want to lose.

Now answer the following questions. The answers are given at the end of the questions.

1. Of the three conversations above, identify which were presented by a Messenger and which were presented by an Advocate.

_____

_____

_____

_____

_____

_____

_____

_____

_____

2. Try to identify what *feelings* or impressions you gained from the conversation with Jake. What type of person did Jake seem to be? How did he approach you? Did he show you respect as the leader of the change programme?

_____

_____

_____

_____

_____

_____

_____

_____

_____

_____

_____

_____

_____

_____

3. Try to identify what *feelings* or impressions you gained from the conversation with Erica. What type of person did Erica seem to be? How did she approach you? Did she show you respect as the leader of the change programme? Did she reflect any other impression she had of you?

_____

_____

_____

_____

_____

_____

_____

_____

_____

_____

_____

_____

_____

_____

_____

4. Try to identify what *feelings* or impressions you gained from the conversation with Gina. What type of person did Gina seem to be? How did she approach you? Did she show you respect as the leader of the change programme? Did she reflect any other impression she had of you or of herself?

_____

_____

_____

_____

_____

_____

_____

_____

_____

_____

_____

_____

_____

_____

Answers

1. The conversation held with Erica represents that of Messenger. She has approached you on behalf of her receptionists, but has effectively 'handed this over' to you for resolution rather than intending to be involved. The conversations with both Jake and Gina represent those of Advocates. Both Jake and Gina are representing people, and obviously intend to revert to the people with feedback.

2. Reading through the conversation between yourself and Jake could possibly have created a number of feelings, interpretations or intuitions for you. Most people with Asperger's will struggle to identify exactly what it is that they are experiencing and as a result misinterpret face-to-face interactions. The questions provided can help you get to the foundation of your reaction to someone.

   What type of person did Jake seem to be? Most people would answer that Jake seemed to be the kind of person who was genuinely concerned about his colleagues.

   How did he approach you? Jake was polite in greeting you and asking if he was able to speak with you, and he also acknowledged that you were possibly busy. His conversation indicates that he felt you were the type of person who would want to know what was being discussed amongst the team.

   Did he show you respect as the leader of the change programme? I would say that the answer to that is yes. He respected your time and your accountability for the success of the programme by bringing the issue to your attention. He also indicated to the employees that he felt you were the type of person who would advise them if there were any potential redundancies – an open indication of respect and belief in you as a leader.

Having considered these questions, it is perhaps easier to recognise that you were probably feeling comfortable with Jake and his approach to you, since he was respectful and supportive.

3. Let's consider the questions in respect of Erica.

   What type of person did Erica seem to be? Most people would answer that Erica seemed to be either nervous or scared or both.

   How did she approach you? Erica phoned you, and then joined you in your office when you invited her. She kept her distance from you and did not sit down until specifically asked to. She only spoke when you prompted her.

   Did she show you respect as the leader of the change programme? I would say that the answer to that is that you cannot really tell from this short conversation. She has brought something to your attention at the request of her receptionists, which indicates respect for them. However, it does not mean she does not respect your role as leader of change, but possibly that she is a bit intimidated by it.

   Did she reflect any other impressions she had of you? If you re-read this conversation, you will see that Erica has tried to keep her distance from you, has avoided eye contact, and has addressed you very formally by your surname. It appears that she may either be intimidated by you or by senior management as a whole. Her immediate reaction when you suggested that the two of you discuss the issue further was to back away and exit (a flight response).

   Having considered these questions, it is perhaps easier to recognise that you were probably feeling uncomfortable during the meeting with Erica. This would have, in all probability, been a subconscious reaction on your part in response to Erica's nervousness.

4. Let's consider the questions in respect of Gina.

   What type of person did Gina seem to be? Most people with Asperger's would answer that Gina seemed to be precise and to the point. Most neurotypicals would probably state that she came across as aggressive. Perhaps reading through the following questions will help you to understand why they would say that.

   How did she approach you? Gina approached you when you were in the middle of a conversation with another member of the leadership team. Apart from being inappropriate, this would generally be taken as rude, since she interrupted a discussion without an apology or acknowledgement to the other person. In addition, she did not approach you in the confidential environment of your office, but in an open area, effectively forcing you to go to your office for the sake of confidentiality.

Did she show you respect as the leader of the change programme? I would say that the answer is no, and there are a few reasons for that. As we have already said, she approached you when you were busy speaking with someone else. That indicates that she felt her conversation was more important than the one you were having. She also did not request a meeting with you, but stated that she needed to talk to you. This type of language would be more appropriate for a supervisor to use to a subordinate, and therefore indicates a lack of respect for your position. Gina forced you to follow her into your office, rather than following you. Again, this is more appropriate behaviour for a supervisor rather than a subordinate. She should have followed your lead.

Did she reflect any other impressions she had of you or herself? Gina refers to herself as part of a group of people who are discontent with the situation, by using the words 'we' and 'our'. By doing this she is distancing herself from you and the decisions of the leadership team. Gina's final comment that the issue is a serious one that needs to be given proper consideration is given in the form of a demand, not a suggestion. It implies that you would not give the issue proper consideration were it not for her highlighting it. She ends with the observation that if the issue is not appropriately addressed, the company will lose key people that it cannot afford to. This is a very thinly concealed threat. 'Address it or else.'

Having considered these questions, it is perhaps easier to recognise that you were probably feeling threatened or annoyed during the meeting with Gina. She is attacking you, indirectly demeaning you and making threats. In all likelihood, her body language would have been uncomfortable for you as well.

Return now to Chapter 21 where negative and positive change agents will be discussed in more detail.

References

Adams, J., Hayes, J. and Hopson, B. (1976) *Transitions: Understanding and Managing Personal Change.* London: Martin Robertson.

Attwood, T. (2007) *The Complete Guide to Asperger's Syndrome.* London: Jessica Kingsley Publishers.

Baddeley, S. and James, K. (1987) 'Owl, Fox, Donkey or Sheep: Political skills for managers.' *Management Education & Development 18*, 1, 3–19.

Baron-Cohen, S. (1995) *Mindblindness: An Essay on Autism and the Theory of Mind.* Cambridge, MA: MIT Press.

Baron-Cohen, S. (2003) *The Essential Difference: Men, Women and the Extreme Male Brain.* London: Penguin.

Beckhard, R. and Harris, R.T. (1987) *Organizational Transitions: Managing Complex Change* (2nd edn). Don Mills, Ontario: Addison-Wesley.

Beckhard, R. and Pritchard, W. (1992) *Changing the Essence: The Art of Creating and Leading Fundamental Change in Organizations.* San Francisco, CA: Jossey-Bass.

Beer, M. (2001) 'How to develop an organization capable of high performance: Embrace the drive for results-capability development paradox.' *Organizational Dynamics 29,* 4, 233–247.

Bergemann, R.A. (2007) *Living and Leading Change: A Hands-on Guide to Change Management.* Cranleigh: Scorpcorp Publishing.

Bridges, W. (1991) *Managing Transitions: Making the Most of Change.* Cambridge, MA: Perseus Books.

Bridges, W. (2000) *The Character of Organizations: Using Personality Type in Organizational Development.* Palo Alto, CA: Davies-Black Publishing.

Buchanan, D. and Boddy, D. (1992) *The Expertise of the Change Agent.* London: Prentice Hall.

Buchanan, D.A. and Badham, R.J. (1999) *Power, Politics and Organizational Change: Winning the Turf Game.* London: Sage.

Clarke, L. (1994) *The Essence of Change.* London: Prentice Hall.

Cooper, R. and Sawaf, A. (1998) *Emotional EQ: Emotional Intelligence in Business.* London: Orion Business.

De Woot, P. (1996) 'Managing change at university.' *Journal of the Association of European Universities, CRE-Action 109*, 19–28.

Doherty, N. (1997) *The Practice of Human Resource Management.* London: Pitman Publishing.

Ekman, P. (2003) *Emotions Revealed.* New York, NY: Times Books.

Forlaron, J. (2005) 'The human side of change leadership.' *Quality Progress 38*, 4, 39–43.

Goleman, D., Boyatzis, R. and McKee, A. (2002) *Primal Leadership: Realizing the Power of Emotional Intelligence.* Boston, MA: Harvard Business School Press.

Gordon, R.M. (1996) '"Radical" Simulationism.' In P. Carruthers and P. Smith (eds) *Theories of Theories of Mind.* Cambridge: Cambridge University Press.

Guest, D.E., Conway, N., Briner, R. and Dickman, N. (1996) *The State of the Psychological Contract in Employment.* London: Institute of Personnel and Development.

Guest, D.E., Peccei, R. and Thomas, A. (1994) *Safety culture of safety performance: British Rail in the aftermath of the Clapham Junction disaster.* Paper presented at the 1994 Occupational Psychology Conference, Birmingham.

Hargie, O. and Tourish, D. (2000) *Handbook of Communication Audits for Organisations.* London: Routledge.

Hayes, J. (2007) *The Theory and Practice of Change Management* (2nd edn). Basingstoke: Palgrave Macmillan.

Hiltrop, J.M. (1996) 'Managing the changing psychological contract.' *Employee Relations 18,* 1, 26–49.

Hofstede, G. (1991) *Cultures and Organizations: Software of the Mind.* London: McGraw-Hill.

Jaskolka, A. (2011) *The Picture Book of Body Language: The Only Language in Which People Can't Lie.* Slough: Foulsham.

Kotter, J.P. (1996) *Leading Change.* Boston, MA: Harvard Business School Press.

Kübler-Ross, E. (1969) *On Death and Dying.* New York, NY: Macmillan.

LaFasto, F. and Larson, C. (2001) *When Teams Work Best.* Beverly Hills, CA: Sage.

Louis, M.R. (1985) 'An Investigator's Guide to Working-place Culture.' In P.J. Frost, L.F. Moore, M.R. Louis, C.C. Lundberg and J. Martin (eds) *Organizational Culture.* Beverly Hills, CA: Sage.

Mabey, C. and Mayon-White, B. (eds) (1993) *Managing Change* (2nd edn). London: Paul Chapman Publishing.

Menkes, J. (2005) 'Hiring for smarts.' *Harvard Business Review 83,* 11, 100–109.

Morgan, G. (1997) *Images of Organization.* London: Sage.

Morrison, E.W. and Milliken, F.J. (2000) 'Organizational silence: A barrier to change and development in a pluralistic world.' *Academy of Management Review 25,* 4, 706–725.

Mullins, L.J. (1999) *Management and Organisational Behaviour* (5th edn). London: Financial Times/Pitman Publishing.

Murrie, D., Lester, M. and Lawson, W. (2005) 'Asperger syndrome in forensic settings.' *International Journal of Forensic Mental Health 1,* 59–70.

Nadler, D.A. (1993) 'Concepts for the Management of Organizational Change.' In C. Mabey and B. Mayon-White (eds) *Managing Change* (2nd edn). London: Paul Chapman Publishing.

Navarro, J. and Karlins, M. (2008) *What Every BODY Is Saying: An Ex-FBI Agent's Guide to Speed-reading People.* New York, NY: HarperCollins.

Pease, A. and Pease, B. (2006) *The Definitive Book of Body Language.* London: Orion.

Pugh, D. (1993) 'Understanding and Managing Organizational Change.' In C. Mabey and B. Mayon-White (eds) *Managing Change* (2nd edn). London: Paul Chapman Publishing.

Reiches, A.E. and Schneider, B. (1990) 'Climate and Culture: An Evolution of Constructs.' In B. Schneider (ed.) *Organizational Climate and Culture.* San Francisco, CA: Jossey-Bass.

Rubin, I. (1987) 'Increasing self-acceptance: A means of reducing prejudice.' *Journal of Personality and Social Psychology 5,* 233–238.

Sackmann, S.A. (1991) *Cultural Knowledge in Organisations: Exploring the Collective Mind.* Newbury Park: Sage.

Satir, V., Gomori, M., Banmen, J. and Gerber, J.S. (1991) *The Satir Model: Family Therapy and Beyond.* Palo Alto, CA: Science and Behavior Books.

Schein, E.H. (1988) *Organizational Psychology* (3rd edn). New York, NY: Prentice Hall.

Schein, E.H. (2004) *Organizational Culture and Leadership.* San Francisco, CA: Jossey-Bass.

Schön, D.A. (1971) *Beyond the Stable State. The 1970 Reith Lectures.* London: Maurice Temple-Smith.

Sims, R.R. (1994) 'Human resource management's role in clarifying the new psychological contract.' *Human Resource Management 33*, 3, 373–382.

Spindler, G.S. (1994) 'Psychological contracts in the workplace: A lawyer's view.' *Human Resource Management 33*, 3, 325–333.

Stein, S.J. and Book, H.E. (2000) *The EQ Edge: Emotional Intelligence and Your Success.* Toronto, Ontario: Multi-Health Systems.

Tichy, N.M. (1982) 'Managing change strategically: The technical, political and cultural keys.' *Organizational Dynamics 4*, 59–80.

Vrij, A. (2000) *Detecting Lies and Deceit.* Chichester: Wiley.

Walters, S.R. (2000) *The Truth about Lying: How to Spot a Lie and Protect Yourself from Deception.* Naperville, IL: Sourcebook.

Weinberg, G. (1997) *Quality Software Management: Vol. 4. Anticipating Change.* New York, NY: Dorset House.

Wilpert, B. (1996) 'Management as a Risk Factor in High Hazard Systems.' In P.J.D. Drenth, P.L. Koopman and B. Wilpert (eds) *Organizational Decision-making under Different Economic and Political Conditions.* Amsterdam: Koninklijke Nederlandse Akademie van Wetenschappen.

Index

Printed in Great Britain
by Amazon